# The Borderline Personality Disorder Survival Guide

## Everything You Need to Know About Living with BPD

Alexander L. Chapman, Ph.D
Kim L. Gratz, Ph.D

EasyRead Large

# Copyright Page from the Original Book

Distributed in Canada by Raincoast Books

Copyright © 2007 by Alexander L. Chapman, Ph.D. and Kim L. Gratz, Ph.D.
New Harbinger Publications, Inc.
5674 Shattuck Avenue
Oakland, CA 94609
www.newharbinger.com

All Rights Reserved
Printed in the United States of America

Acquired by Catharine Sutker; Cover design by Amy Shoup;
Edited by Karen O'Donnell Stein; Text design by Tracy Carlson

Library of Congress Cataloging-in-Publication Data

Chapman, Alexander L. (Alexander Lawrence)
  The borderline personality disorder survival guide : everything you need to know about living with BPD / Alexander L. Chapman & Kim L. Gratz.
    p. cm.
  Includes bibliographical references.
  ISBN-13: 978-1-57224-507-5 (trade paper : alk. paper)
  ISBN-10: 1-57224-507-7 (trade paper : alk. paper)
  1. Borderline personality disorder--Popular works. I. Gratz, Kim L. II. Title.
  RC569.5.B67C475 2007
  616.85'852--dc22
                                        2007037975

09 08 07
10 9 8 7 6 5 4 3 2 1                    First printing

## TABLE OF CONTENTS

| | |
|---|---|
| Publisher's Note | i |
| Foreword | iv |
| Acknowledgments | ix |
| Introduction: Orientation and User's Guide | xiii |

### PART 1: WHAT IS BORDERLINE PERSONALITY DISORDER?

| | |
|---|---|
| 1: What Is Borderline Personality Disorder? | 3 |
| 2: Borderline Personality Disorder: Is What They Say Really True? | 35 |
| 3: What Causes Borderline Personality Disorder? | 61 |
| 4: Will I Have Borderline Personality Disorder Forever? The Course of BPD | 101 |
| 5: Problems That Often Go Along with Borderline Personality Disorder | 132 |
| 6: Suicidal Behavior and Deliberate Self-Harm | 166 |

### PART 2: How Do I Get Help for BPD?

| | |
|---|---|
| 7: How Do I Find Help for Borderline Personality Disorder? | 203 |
| 8: Dialectical Behavior Therapy | 235 |
| 9: Mentalization-Based Treatment | 278 |
| 10: Medication Treatments | 305 |
| 11: Dealing with Suicidal Thoughts | 355 |
| 12: Coping with Your Emotions | 377 |
| References | 407 |

# Publisher's Note

*Care has been taken to confirm the accuracy of the information presented and to describe generally accepted practices. However, the authors, editors, and publisher are not responsible for errors or omissions or for any consequences from application of the information in this book and make no warranty, express or implied, with respect to the contents of the publication.*

*The authors, editors, and publisher have exerted every effort to ensure that any drug selection and dosage set forth in this text are in accordance with current recommendations and practice at the time of publication. However, in view of ongoing research, changes in government regulations, and the constant flow of information relating to drug therapy and drug reactions, the reader is urged to check the package insert for each drug for any change in indications and dosage and for added warnings and precautions. This is particularly important when the recommended agent is a new or infrequently employed drug.*

*Some drugs and medical devices presented in this publication may have Food and Drug Administration (FDA) clearance for limited use in restricted research settings. It is the responsibility of the health care provider to ascertain the FDA status of each drug or device planned for use in their clinical practice.*

To those who struggle with borderline personality disorder. To my wonderful wife, Katherine, and my son, Max.
—ALC

To all of my clients, whose courageous struggles with BPD have inspired and taught me so much. I wish you peace, love, and self-compassion.
—KLG

# Foreword

The borderline personality disorder community is well served with this comprehensive guide by Dr. Alex Chapman and Dr. Kim Gratz, *The Borderline Personality Disorder Survival Guide: Everything You Need to Know About Living with BPD.*

Key in the coming of age of all illnesses, medical or psychiatric, is the dissemination of current information. BPD is no exception. But the considerable controversy and confusion surrounding BPD make for a challenge in educating people about the disorder that goes beyond the multiple challenges of the disorder itself. Drs. Chapman and Gratz have met the task head-on.

One can sense the intensive discussions that must have accompanied this joint undertaking; it is no simple feat to present complex issues in a highly readable yet medically sound work. This collaboration offers readers up-to-date, research-based information and addresses the controversies in a clear and direct way. The authors' respectful tone is consistent throughout each well-defined chapter. This respect for their reader and passion for their topic has generated a book *for* the sufferers, not *about* the sufferers. The conversational style brings an immediacy that masks the depth of the authors' thinking. This stance has skillfully ensured that the book will serve a wide audience. It provides a breadth of information that makes it an excellent resource for others affected by BPD. Achieving such balance makes *The Borderline Personality Disorder Survival Guide* a valued handbook for the entire BPD community: people with BPD, family members, and clinicians.

The word "guide" in the title sums up the purpose of the book: to provide a BPD road map. From the start, the reader is oriented to the journey. The first part provides information and data on BPD, while the second outlines treatment recommendations, with both sections offering education and practical, hands-on support. In chapter 1, for example, the reader is given "a clear, easily understandable picture of BPD."

With this picture also come words of caution urging the reader to seek professional consultation for an accurate assessment and, thus, not to jump to conclusions. The reader is then referred to chapter 7, which lists appropriate steps in locating help. This kind of equilibrium permeates the book. The authors offer guidance and then explain how to carry out the recommendations.

This balanced approach extends to the discussion of the cause of the disorder, an issue that often creates great controversy. Drs. Chapman and Gratz write that, along with biological factors, stressful life experiences can be involved. Their nonjudgmental stance neither ignores nor vilifies the impact of parenting. For example, consider the concept of the invalidating environment proposed by Marsha M. Linehan, Ph.D. An invalidating environment at home or at school (including encounters with family members and peers) can be as relevant to the development of BPD as severe sexual or physical abuse; nothing ever should minimize such invalidating experiences. However, supported by cited research, the authors duly note that this type of environment alone is not sufficient to cause BPD and, therefore, other factors need to be taken into account. Similarly, again with a no-blame attitude, the authors note that exact factors that promote and further the disorder cannot be pinpointed, but they identify and delineate several theories.

Drs. Chapman and Gratz provide research references throughout the book, ensuring that readers have access to evidence-based information. In the chapter on medication—often a confusing issue—they give the reader a pros-and-cons model. Not only is the research outlined, there is psychoeducation on topics such as types of studies and the use of placebos. This user-friendly chapter makes a complicated subject more manageable, enabling the reader to make educated and informed decisions.

The book's lively, interactive sense is in part due to the examples and metaphors and the stories of people with BPD. These give images that are readily understood and can be felt by the reader. There is compassion and empathy here, as well as extensive expertise.

Drs. Chapman and Gratz are both accomplished researchers and experts in the treatment of BPD. As a result, in this book, they blend scientific information with their hands-on experience, resulting in information and examples that will resonate with a broad audience. Of note, both authors have received the Young Investigator's Award from the National Education Alliance for BPD (Dr. Gratz in 2005; Dr. Chapman in 2007) for their stellar contributions to the research and treatment of BPD.

Drs. Chapman and Gratz deserve hearty congratulations. They have provided a rightful balance between hope and long-term concerns for those affected by this difficult disorder. Their style is empowering in all twelve chapters in this book, and they address the most salient topics on a difficult but highly treatable disorder.

—Perry D. Hoffman, Ph.D.

# Acknowledgments

I would like to acknowledge the encouragement, support, and mentoring of several people. First, I am grateful for the wisdom and support of Marsha Linehan, who has helped me to step onto the right path, and whose tireless work in developing treatments for BPD has helped countless people around the world. I thank my graduate-school mentors, Richard Farmer and Tony Cellucci, for providing invaluable support and guidance in my research and clinical work in the area of BPD. I thank Tom Lynch for showing me how to go beyond my comfort level as a therapist and Clive Robins for his uncanny ability to size up and simplify complicated problems. I am very grateful for my continued friendships and collaborations with Marsha, Rich, Tony, Tom, and Clive.

This book would certainly not have been possible without the efforts of several people. I feel fortunate to have worked with Kim Gratz. When the opportunity to write the book came up,

Kim's name came quickly to mind, and thanks to her labors, this book is much better than it would have been without them. I look forward to our continued collaborations. I also express my sincere appreciation for the efforts and support of Karen Stein, Catharine Sutker, and Jess Beebe, at New Harbinger Publications. They have helped us improve our work, and I have greatly appreciated their enthusiasm for this book, especially as our looming deadline approached. I am also continually grateful to my clients for inviting me into their lives. I sincerely hope that this book will help some people find their way out of the dark and into a life that is satisfying and fulfilling.

I also appreciate the continued support and enthusiasm of my parents and my wife, Katherine. She and my son, Max, have had to put up with my absence on far too many Saturdays while I wrote this book. With the continued love and support of my family, I truly live a charmed life.

—Alex Chapman

This book would not have been possible without the encouragement, support, and guidance of many people in my life. First, I would like to thank my mentors in the area of BPD, Elizabeth Murphy and John Gunderson. Elizabeth's support kept me grounded, and her enthusiasm and remarkable skill reinforced my passion for and commitment to this work. She remains one of the most inspiring clinicians I know. John's mentoring introduced me to different perspectives and expanded my worldview, both of which have been invaluable in my growth as a researcher and clinician. I will always be grateful for the opportunities he provided and the experiences I had while working with him. I would also like to thank Liz Roemer, my mentor in all things academic, for her continued emotional and intellectual support.

    I would like to thank my colleague and coauthor, Alex Chapman, for inviting me to join him in writing this book. It was an amazingly positive process, and I am grateful for our continued collaboration. Thanks are also due to Karen Stein and the people at New Harbinger Publications, especially Catharine Sutker and Jess Beebe, for their tireless efforts and support. In addition, I am eternally grateful to the clients whose strength and courage prompted me to pursue research and clinical work in this area. They taught me more than any book ever could, and showed me the wisdom in their behaviors. I thank them for being a part of my life and for allowing me to share in their recovery process.

On a personal note, I would like to thank my parents for their unconditional love, validation, and accurate mirroring. Without this support throughout my life, I could not have made it this far. Last, but certainly not least, I would like to thank Matt Tull, my ever-supportive husband. His support grounds me, his encouragement motivates me, and his passion for clinical psychology inspires me. Also, his willingness to read and edit numerous drafts of this manuscript undoubtedly made it a better product. I am eternally grateful to share my life with him.

—Kim L. Gratz

# Introduction: Orientation and User's Guide

*Jane was fourteen years old when she first cut herself. That morning had started off as a pretty normal one. Jane had gone to school and hung out with some friends. During lunch, her friend Randy had been teasing her about her recent breakup with her boyfriend ("Jane, it looks like you're not cut out to have a boyfriend. Maybe you should get a cat!"). On her way home, Jane couldn't stop thinking about Randy's comments. As she walked, she became increasingly scared, ashamed, and angry. With each step, Jane felt as if she were losing herself, and she feared that she would never be able to stop feeling like this. By the time she got home, she was so overwhelmed that she pushed past her parents, rushed up to her room, locked her door, and desperately tried to figure out a way to release her feelings before she exploded. She couldn't come up with anything that would help, and she impulsively grabbed a shard of glass from a cup she had accidentally broken the day before.*

People with borderline personality disorder (BPD) struggle with their emotions, their behaviors, and their sense of identity, as well as their relationships with other people. Because they are in such emotional turmoil, they often resort to coping strategies that seem to work in the moment but actually make their problems worse (such as suicide attempts, self-harm, or drug use). Indeed, people with BPD sometimes careen through life as if they're driving a 350-horsepower car with no brakes. They often act on the spur of the moment without thinking things through carefully. As a result, their relationships and responsibilities may suffer. Emotionally, people with BPD are like burn victims (Linehan 1993a), extremely sensitive to even the slightest hint of an emotion and yet so afraid of their emotions that they seek to do anything and everything they can to avoid them.

BPD has received an explosion of interest lately, both from researchers and the popular media. Researchers are examining what causes BPD, when and how people recover from BPD, the brain areas involved in BPD, and the treatments that help people with BPD lead fulfilling and satisfying lives. In the past couple of years alone, articles in both the *New York Times* and *O, the Oprah Magazine* featured Dr. Marsha Linehan's groundbreaking work on dialectical behavior therapy for BPD (Linehan 1993a). What's more, popular movies, such as *Girl, Interrupted,* have featured characters with BPD, and television shows, such as *Beverly Hills 90210* and *7th Heaven,* have featured characters who injure themselves, a symptom that sometimes occurs in BPD.

You might be asking yourself, "Why is BPD such a hot topic now?" A better question is "What took so long?" People with BPD experience intense emotional pain. They struggle with unrelenting chaos in their relationships with other people; feelings of emptiness, aloneness, and desperation; and a confused sense of who they are and where they are going in life. Indeed, up to 10 percent of people with BPD commit suicide, a rate that is over fifty times that of the general population (Skodol et al. 2002). Yet, despite all of this, many people with BPD do not receive the support they need.

BPD also influences the lives of family members, friends, and caregivers. If a chemist were to concoct a potion that would create stress, concern, and heartbreak among loved ones, this potion would probably look a lot like BPD. It is heartbreaking and scary when someone you love talks about or attempts suicide. Trying to help someone with BPD overcome emotional turmoil is like being dropped into a fighter jet going full speed and not knowing how or where to land it.

The powerful emotions and sensitivity of people with BPD can be exciting and intense. People with BPD can be dramatic and charismatic, and they are often quite caring and understanding. Nevertheless, caring for someone with BPD is like trying to hold onto the sun: the emotional intensity of a person with BPD can singe and char relationships. Further, people with BPD often become swallowed by grief or sadness, leaving the caregiver or family member in the dark about what to do.

Many people with BPD and their loved ones do not know how to understand the difficulties they struggle with on a daily basis, or where to turn for help. Although there is a smattering of information available online, the Internet can be a confusing and treacherous place for someone who is suffering, with misinformation and websites offering dangerous advice (such as those that promote self-harm and eating-disordered behaviors) lurking around every corner.

Where else can someone with BPD go to get useful information? Two sources that contain a lot of information are treatment manuals and research papers. However, these sources can be very difficult to use and understand if you are not a therapist or a researcher, and especially if you don't have a therapist or someone with expertise to help you.

It is critical for people struggling with BPD to have up-to-date, accurate, and accessible information on the problems they are facing and on where to turn to get help. Therefore, we wrote this book, in order to give people with BPD an easy-to-follow road map to guide them through the maze of their problems. This book will be especially helpful if any of the following statements describe you:

- You have been diagnosed with BPD and want to learn more about the disorder.
- You think that you may have BPD and want to figure out what to do.
- You harm yourself, experience emotional turmoil, and want to learn helpful coping skills.
- You are in therapy or take medications and want to learn more about BPD, its causes, and the things you can do to help yourself.
- You care for or treat someone with BPD, and you want a comprehensible source of information that tells you exactly what BPD is all about.

# How to Navigate This Book

Throughout this book, we answer many questions you might have if you struggle with BPD or similar problems. For instance, there is a lot of confusion about the term *borderline personality disorder.* In chapter 1, we describe what we mean by this term and where the idea for this disorder came from in the first place. We also describe how mental health professionals diagnose people with BPD. We hope this chapter will provide you with the information you need in order to understand the nature of BPD.

Unfortunately (and this is probably not news to you), mental health problems carry a huge social stigma. In the days of the ancient Greeks, people with mental health problems were seen as having an imbalance of bodily fluids (too much "black bile," for example). From the Middle Ages through the nineteenth century, people attributed mental illness to poor moral character, demonic possession, or other factors. As late as the 1800s, people believed that abnormalities in the shape of the skull caused mental illness (it's true—there was an entire field of study devoted to skull shapes, called *phrenology*). Although we are now more sophisticated in our thinking about mental illness, people who act in a way that is different from what society thinks of as "normal" are often rejected, ostracized, and judged. This is true not only for people with mental illness but also for those with differences in racial or ethnic identity, sexual orientation, and cultural or religious practices.

Social stigma definitely affects those with BPD. Many of the problems that go along with having BPD strike a nerve with people in Western culture. For instance, if you have BPD, you might have more difficulty than the average person does when your relationships end. You might even try desperately to stop other people from leaving you. This behavior, although understandable, can rub others the wrong way, because many people in our society have been taught to value independence and to look negatively upon people who are "too dependent." Suicidal and self-harm behaviors are often incredibly shocking, scary, and puzzling to people who have never had experience with these behaviors. Society also rejects people who use a lot of drugs or alcohol, get too angry, express emotions too strongly, or seem "out of control." Unfortunately, this is the same mix of problems that often goes along with BPD. As a result, sometimes the very people they turn to for help (family, friends, and even therapists) reject people with BPD. We feel strongly that there is a need to combat the stigma associated with BPD. We have devoted chapter 2 to challenging myths about BPD and (we hope) reducing stigma.

If you struggle with BPD or know someone who does, you probably have many questions about what causes these problems in the first place. Indeed, it is important to be knowledgeable about the causes of your problems. If you were a cancer patient, you would want to know exactly how you got cancer and what the best treatment might be. Fortunately, researchers have focused lots of time and energy on learning more about the causes of BPD, and some answers are starting to emerge. In general, we now know that people develop BPD from a combination of heredity, personality traits related to emotionality or impulsivity, and stressful events experienced while growing up. In chapter 3, we discuss some likely causes of BPD.

When you are struggling, it is essential to have hope that things will improve in the future. Unfortunately, the term *personality disorder* does nothing to foster hope! This term makes it sound like you've got a black spot on your soul that will never be removed. Fortunately, we know that this is not true. Research findings have indicated that people with BPD can and do get better over time (zanarini et al. 2003). What's more, with treatment, people with BPD can make amazing changes in their lives. In chapter 4, we summarize the current knowledge about the recovery time for those with BPD, as well as which symptoms seem to get better over time and which ones tend to stick around.

Now, one important thing to keep in mind about BPD is that it comes with a lot of extra baggage. That is, many people with BPD have other problems and may meet criteria for other diagnoses. For instance, many people with BPD suffer from depression, anxiety disorders, eating disorders, and/or drug and alcohol problems. People with BPD are also at risk for suicide attempts, self-harm, and other self-destructive behaviors. In chapters 5 and 6, we describe and discuss the problems that go along with having BPD.

In part 2 of this book, we change our focus. Part 1 (chapters 1 through 6) focuses on providing information about BPD, but part 2 is intended to help you figure out how to get help for BPD. We know that when you are suffering, struggling with overwhelming emotions, and dealing with a seemingly unending barrage of problems on a daily basis, it can be difficult to figure out how to get help. Part 2 will assist you in the process of finding the help you need. One of the best ways to do this is to seek help from a mental health professional who treats people with BPD (or the problems that go along with BPD). In chapter 7, we give you concrete suggestions and practical information on how to find people who can make sense of your problems and suggest a course of action. We also explain what to expect from therapy, should you choose to go.

Of course, while you are seeking help for BPD or any other condition, it is important to be aware of the treatment options, and to know what treatments seem to work best. For instance, it is common knowledge that antibiotics work best for bacterial illnesses and are not advisable for viral illnesses. If you were suffering from viral pneumonia, and your doctor prescribed antibiotics, you would want to know that this might not be the best treatment for you. Similarly, you'll need to know which BPD treatments are most useful. In chapters 8 and 9, we discuss a couple of psychological treatments that have been found to help people with BPD (dialectical behavior therapy and mentalization-based treatment). Then, in chapter 10, we describe common medications used to treat BPD, and we discuss how well these medications seem to work. We also provide some guidance regarding making decisions about medications, questions to ask your physician, and how to monitor whether your medication is working.

Whether you are already in treatment, seeking treatment, or fed up with your current treatment, you may want to know about some coping skills that help people with BPD. In chapters 11 and 12, we describe coping skills that can be very helpful to you. Remember that self-help alone is probably not enough to enable you to overcome your life problems; however, practicing some useful coping skills can help you to manage your emotions (chapter 12) and stay alive (chapter 11 deals with suicidal thoughts) as you explore your treatment options.

As you read the above-described chapters, you'll notice that we have included some examples of people who have struggled with problems related to BPD. Some of these examples are hypothetical, and others are based on our own experiences with people who have BPD. When we have included examples based on actual individuals, we have modified the information in order to protect the individuals' identities.

We wrote this book as a guide to help people with BPD understand and get help for their problems. You may find that starting at the beginning and reading through to the end is the most helpful way to use the book. That way, you will learn all about BPD before you read about how to seek help and cope with some of your problems. But you could also use it as you would a user's manual, by checking out certain sections for information as needed. We hope that this book provides you with the information you need to tackle the problems that go along with BPD, so you can move forward in your life, heading in the directions that are most important to you.

# PART 1
# WHAT IS BORDERLINE PERSONALITY DISORDER?

# 1
# What Is Borderline Personality Disorder?

*Wendy walked through the door to the therapist's office. She was ready to make a change in her life. She couldn't go on living like this any longer. Although she was incredibly sensitive, intelligent, and kind, Wendy had been living her life as if she were behind the wheel of a huge truck, careening through neighborhoods, driving over lawns, and crashing into lampposts. She had looked up borderline personality disorder on the Internet and was ready to find out whether this was the problem she'd been struggling with for so long.*

We have devoted this chapter to giving you a clear, easily understandable picture of BPD. If you think that you or someone close to you might have BPD, it is helpful to know exactly what this means. In this chapter, we describe the features and symptoms of BPD. We clarify exactly what *borderline personality disorder* means, describe each of the nine different symptoms that are part of this disorder, and explain how professionals diagnose this disorder. We also provide some information on the history of BPD.

Before you start reading this chapter, it is important for you to know that you can't diagnose yourself with BPD. Although you might read about some of the symptoms of BPD and think "That's me!" you must see a professional (a psychologist, a psychiatrist, or someone else who diagnoses psychiatric disorders) to figure out whether you actually have BPD. Trying to diagnose yourself with a psychiatric disorder is much like trying to diagnose yourself with cancer or heart disease. You need a professional to do it, because you most likely don't have the tools, skills, or objective viewpoint necessary to make the diagnosis. Moreover, if you made the wrong diagnosis, you might not get the right kind of help.

We have met with several people who thought they had BPD but turned out to have some other disorder, like depression, bipolar disorder, or post-traumatic stress disorder. Just as the recommended treatments for cancer are different from those for heart disease, each psychological or emotional disorder requires a different treatment. Therefore, you'll need to make sure your diagnosis is accurate, and the only way to do this is to see a professional. So, use this chapter to learn what BPD is all about and to get a better understanding of the symptoms of this disorder. Then, if you want to figure out whether you have BPD, go and see someone who can make a professional diagnosis. See chapter 7 for guidance on how to do this.

# Psychiatric Disorders, Personality Disorders, and BPD

The *Diagnostic and Statistical Manual of Mental Disorders* (*DSM-IV-TR*; American Psychiatric Association 2000) is like a recipe book used by mental health professionals that lists the essential ingredients for particular psychological or emotional problems. Within this recipe book are two main types of psychiatric disorders: clinical disorders and personality disorders. According to the *DSM-IV-TR,* BPD is a psychiatric disorder that fits within a larger category of personality disorders.

## *Clinical Disorders*

One type of psychiatric disorder is a *clinical disorder* or *syndrome.* Examples of these disorders include depression, anxiety disorders (such as panic disorder, generalized anxiety disorder, or social anxiety disorder), and schizophrenia. These disorders are seen as syndromes that people develop at various points in their lives. Some of these disorders may last for only a short period and have symptoms that improve quite quickly with treatment (such as panic disorder), whereas others are generally more long lasting and debilitating (such as schizophrenia).

## Personality Disorders

The other main type of psychiatric disorder is a *personality disorder.* So, what is a personality disorder? The idea here is that we all have typical ways of acting, feeling, thinking, and relating to the world, which make up our personality. Whenever you say "He (or she) is a real character!" you are really referring to that person's personality, or typical way of acting or relating to the world. A personality disorder is simply a long-lasting pattern of relating to the world that doesn't work very well. In addition, these problems cause great distress and may create difficulties in relationships or lead to problems reaching goals in life (such as goals involving getting or keeping a desired job). There are many different types of personality disorders, including avoidant, obsessive-compulsive, dependent, paranoid, schizoid, schizotypal, narcissistic, histrionic, antisocial, and, of course, borderline personality disorder.

Having a personality disorder usually means having a set of problems that have been with you for a long time. Generally, you have to be an adult to be diagnosed with a personality disorder. However, people diagnosed with personality disorders as adults will often say that they have struggled with these problems for as long as they can remember. Therefore, we believe that many people have had these problems since they were children. Having a personality disorder *does not* mean that you have a flawed personality, possess poor character, or are a mean or unlikable person.

Basically, the assumption is that people with personality disorders have something in their personalities that creates problems for them and for other people. Now, we don't entirely agree with this, for a few reasons. First, the term *personality disorder* is problematic, because it's often used interchangeably with phrases like "character flaw," "problem person," and "difficult personality," and, as we said before, this usage is not accurate. Second, this term suggests that the problem is inside of you, and that if you could only fix yourself everything would be normal.

We disagree with this viewpoint as well. There is a lot of evidence that the environment (such as stress, trauma, abuse, and other such factors) plays a strong role in many psychological problems, including personality disorders. In addition, placing the problem inside of you can create stigma and judgmental reactions on the part of other people.

Finally, the term *personality disorder* also suggests that, if you have a personality disorder, you have always had it (it's part of your personality, part of what makes you the person you are) and you always will have it. As you'll see in chapter 4, however, there is evidence that BPD doesn't always last as long as people think it does. So, having BPD does not mean that you have a flawed personality, or that you will always struggle with the problems you are having right now. It simply means that you have a pattern of thinking, feeling, and behaving that may be hindering your ability to have a high quality of life, keep your relationships going strong, or reach your goals.

Complicating matters is the fact that the *DSM-IV-TR* is based partly on the idea that psychiatric disorders are much like medical illnesses or diseases. The *DSM-IV-TR* uses a "disease model" for psychological disorders, relating them to some kind of pathology (dysfunction) within the individual (or in the environment), much like you would with pneumonia, diabetes, or other such diseases.

The problem with this idea is that psychiatric disorders do not seem to operate in the same way as diseases do. First, you can't "catch" a psychiatric disorder like you can catch pneumonia. Second, unlike diseases such as diabetes, psychiatric disorders have not been linked to any physical malfunction that might cause them. Third, many of the symptoms of specific disorders (such as depression) are also found in many other disorders, so the line between these disorders is blurry. In contrast, it is very clear to physicians when a person has diabetes versus breast cancer. Fourth, diagnoses are based on what you do, think, or feel. The assumption is that certain things that you might do, think, or feel would indicate the presence of some kind of underlying disorder. That's a pretty big leap to make. Scientists can't look inside someone's body or brain and find an underlying disorder, like they do when they discover a cancerous tumor. Fifth, the disease model, like the term *personality disorder,* places the problem mostly inside of you. As we describe below, if you have BPD, many of the problems that you struggle with are related to problems in the environment, rather than problems that exist inside of you. Moreover, the changes that you might have to make in order to be happier may actually involve changing the environment or changing how you behave, think, or feel. Therefore, we believe that what you do, think, and feel are much more important than whether you have some kind of disorder.

## *Where Did BPD Come From? The History of BPD*

It is important to know a little about the history of what is now called BPD.

In the nineteenth century, people used the word *borderline* to describe a condition that existed on the fuzzy border between two different types of psychiatric problems (Stone 2005).

The widely held view was that there were two large categories of psychiatric disorders or problems. One category, called *neurosis,* involved patients who were aware of reality but who had emotional problems, such as depression or anxiety disorders. The other category, *psychosis,* involved patients who had unusual thoughts and experiences (such as hallucinations) that were not based in reality, and these patients were diagnosed with disorders such as schizophrenia. Patients who didn't have problems serious enough to be labeled psychotic (in other words, their thinking and experiences were largely based in reality), but were too troubled to be called neurotic were put into the borderline category. Psychiatrists used the term *borderline* for patients who had a hard time seeing both the good and bad qualities in people at the same time, who led unstable and chaotic lives, and who were often emotionally distraught (Stone 2005). Many of these ways of thinking about BPD came directly from observations of a limited number of patients and were not based on scientific research.

Since those early days, researchers have conducted numerous studies. Findings from these studies have identified many important characteristics that make up what we now call *borderline personality disorder,* including difficulties managing emotions, impulsive behavior, and relationship and identity problems. People with BPD are no longer thought to be bordering on psychosis and neurosis. Science is helping us keep the ideas about BPD that seem to be true and discard the old ideas about BPD that do not seem to be accurate.

# The Symptoms and Features of Borderline Personality Disorder

*Wendy had known for a long time that there was simply something different about her. She remembered that she was an extremely emotional young child. It seemed like she was always crying or getting excited about things that other people were not getting excited about. Although she has a great deal of empathy for others, her trouble in dealing with her emotions upsets her and has caused some problems in her life, leading to conflicts in her relationships and making it hard for her to keep a job.*

BPD is a disorder of instability and problems with emotions. People with BPD are unstable in their emotions, their thinking, their relationships, their identity, and their behavior. People with BPD have rocky relationships and are often afraid of being abandoned. Emotionally, people with BPD feel like they are on a roller coaster, with their emotions going up and down at the drop of a hat. They may also have trouble with anger (either having anger outbursts or being so scared of anger that they avoid it entirely). People with BPD act impulsively (they act quickly without thinking) when they are upset, and they sometimes attempt suicide and engage in self-harm. Often, people with BPD have trouble figuring out who they are, and they sometimes have trouble thinking clearly and staying grounded when they are stressed out. Approximately 1 to 2 percent of people meet the diagnostic criteria for BPD (American Psychiatric Association 2000).

Dr. Marsha Linehan (1993a), who has developed an effective treatment for BPD (dialectical behavior therapy, discussed in chapter 8), has put the nine symptoms of BPD into five easily understandable categories: (1) emotion dysregulation, (2) interpersonal dysregulation, (3) behavioral dysregulation, (4) identity or self dysregulation, and (5) cognitive dysregulation.

You'll notice that the word *dysregulation* pops up in each of these five categories. Dysregulated basically means "not controlled." Indeed, BPD is a disorder that involves being unstable and not controlled in many different areas of life. Below, we expand on these categories and describe the features that fall within them. See table

1.1 for the nine official *DSM-IV-TR* criteria for BPD.

## *Emotion Dysregulation*

*Even as a child, Wendy was extremely emotional and had a hard time managing her emotions. She remembers walking up to the door on the first day of kindergarten, terrified of the other students and frozen in place. Now, as an adult, Wendy sometimes feels so irritable and agitated that even the slightest annoyance (such as being stuck behind a slow driver or having to wait in line) grates on her, like the sound of nails scratching a chalkboard. Despite her best efforts, she sometimes loses control of her anger, exploding in an angry outburst. These outbursts have alienated her from other people, led to problems in her job, and left her feeling ashamed, guilty, and empty.*

Emotion dysregulation refers to unstable emotions (including rapid mood changes) and difficulty managing emotions. People with BPD struggle with their emotions and are often overwhelmed by them. In fact, some researchers have said that emotion dysregulation is the most important problem for people with BPD (Linehan 1993a; Lynch et al. 2006). Indeed, some people believe that most of the problems that people with BPD struggle with are caused by emotion dysregulation. Unstable emotions and moods and difficulty controlling anger are the two symptoms of BPD that fall under this category.

**Unstable Emotions and Moods**

People with BPD often react to things that might not affect other people quite so strongly. For instance, if you have BPD, you might be easily upset by things that people say or do, or you might find that you get stressed out more easily than other people. Just a small critical or disapproving look might be enough to throw you into an emotional tailspin. Because people with BPD react emotionally to so many things, they often find that their emotions go up and down like a roller-coaster ride. They might feel happy one minute, and then sad or angry the next minute.

> ### Table 1.1 A Snapshot of the Diagnostic and Statistical Manual of Mental Disorders (DSM-IV-TR) Criteria for Borderline Personality Disorder
>
> - Frantic efforts to avoid real or imagined abandonment
> - A pattern of intense and unstable interpersonal relationships characterized by alternating between extremes of idealization and devaluation
> - Identity disturbance: markedly and persistently unstable self-image or sense of self
> - Impulsivity in at least two areas that is potentially self-damaging
> - Recurrent suicidal behavior, gestures, or threats, or selfmutilating behavior
> - Affective instability due to a marked reactivity of mood
> - Chronic feelings of emptiness
> - Inappropriate, intense anger or difficulty controlling anger

> • Transient, stress-related paranoid ideation or severe dissociative symptoms
> 
> *Note:* Taken from the *DSM-IV-TR* (American Psychiatric Association 2000).

## Intense Anger or Difficulty Controlling Anger

Intense anger or difficulty controlling anger is another feature of BPD. People with BPD may be very easily irritated or angered by things that might not upset other people. They may also be unable to control themselves when they get angry—throwing things, yelling at people, or feeling so consumed by rage that they don't know what to do. Although anger is one criterion for BPD, we have noticed, in working with people who have BPD, that the emotions of shame, sadness, and guilt are often much stronger and harder to cope with. Some people with BPD seem to spend more time being angry with themselves than with anyone else.

# Interpersonal Dysregulation

*Although she was charming and likable, Wendy often felt like she was on a roller-coaster ride in her relationships with her friends, family members, and people she dated. The slightest hint of criticism or a disapproving look pierced Wendy like a sharp knife. And sometimes, whoever she was dating at the time seemed perfect, and at other times, she couldn't stand to be around him.*

*Interpersonal dysregulation* means having trouble with relationships with other people. It does not mean that you are a bad or unlikable person. In fact, people with BPD are often quite charming, engaging, interesting, and sensitive. Nevertheless, they tend to struggle in their relationships in two primary ways: unstable relationships, and fear of abandonment.

## Unstable and Intense Relationships

People with BPD often have "rocky" relationships that are chaotic and out of control. Indeed, their emotional intensity sometimes makes it hard for them to deal with relationships. If you have BPD, you may find that sometimes things go unbelievably well in your relationships, and at other times everything seems to fall apart. You may be happy, in love, and overjoyed one moment, and the next moment you may feel anger and hatred and have hopeless thoughts about your relationships. The basic idea is that relationships, like emotions, seem like a roller-coaster ride, and they move quickly back and forth between being really good and really bad. If you have BPD, your relationships may also involve many conflicts, fights, and even physical or emotional abuse.

**Frantic Efforts to Avoid Abandonment**

Another feature of BPD is the fear of being abandoned. In fact, some researchers have suggested that fears of abandonment and of being alone are some of the most important problems in BPD (Gunderson 1996). People with BPD often feel panicky and afraid when a relationship with a friend, therapist, intimate partner, or family member is coming to an end. They sometimes think that they are going to be alone forever or that they won't have the support they need to get through their daily struggles. The fear of being alone and of being left can be so intense and troubling that some people with BPD go to great lengths to try to stop people from leaving them. They may beg or plead, try to start a fight (just to make the person stay for a little while longer), or even physically stop the person from leaving.

## *Behavioral Dysregulation*

*Although she was a straight-A student in high school and continued to do very well in college, Wendy dropped out just months before she was to receive her BA (in psychology). When asked why, Wendy replied, "I just couldn't handle the pressure anymore. I didn't see what I was going to do afterward, and the fear was eating me up!" When Wendy got upset, she often acted without thinking and did things that she regretted.*

*She with men she would meet in bars, and sometimes ate so much that she felt like she would vomit. Wendy even tried to kill herself a couple of times to escape the chaos of her life. used alcohol and drugs to numb her pain, had one-night stands*

*Behavioral dysregulation* means that your behavior is out of control (and potentially harmful or risky) and is having a negative effect on your life. People with BPD often struggle with this problem in two primary ways: risky impulsive behavior and self-harm.

## Impulsivity That Can Be Self-Damaging

First, people with BPD take risks that may harm themselves or others. For instance, some people with BPD spend impulsively, drive recklessly, engage in risky sexual activity, binge on food, or have problems with drugs or alcohol. If you have BPD, you might struggle with some or all of these things, too. Maybe you know that these behaviors are not good for you, but you do them anyway, often acting on the spur of the moment and not thinking about what will happen later on. In our experience, people with BPD act impulsively mainly when they are upset, in order to get some temporary relief from their emotional pain.

**Suicidal or Self-Harm Behavior**

Second, another criterion for BPD involves *suicidal behavior* and *deliberate self-harm.* Suicidal behavior involves thinking about suicide, trying to kill oneself, or actually committing suicide. Deliberate self-harm involves self-harm without any intent to cause death. In chapter 6, we talk in much more depth about suicide and deliberate self-harm. For now, just be aware that one of the criteria for a BPD diagnosis is recurrent suicidal behavior, suicide threats, or self-harm.

## *Self and Identity Dysregulation*

*Wendy was always making changes in her life. When she was in college, she was convinced that she wanted to pursue a career in engineering. Then, in her second year, she abruptly changed her major to geography and excelled in all of her geography courses. She soon decided that she hated geography and switched to psychology. After she dropped out of college, she bounced from one type of job (cafe barista) to another (accounting clerk), changed religions (from Catholic to Buddhist) and then denounced religion altogether, and even changed her clothing and appearance weekly (for example, going from a gothic style to a preppy one). She told her therapist that she had no idea who she really was, and that she felt like a completely different person in different situations.*

With *self and identity dysregulation*, a person does not have a clear or stable sense of who he or she is and can also feel empty much of the time.

## Unstable Sense of Self and Identity

People with BPD often have an unstable sense of identity. If you have BPD, you might feel as if your sense of who you are changes a lot, depending on the situation you are in. We all feel and act a little different in different situations. You might act and feel different when you are at work versus when you are home, when you are playing with your children versus when you are going out with friends. But identity disturbance doesn't just involve acting and feeling different; it also involves the feeling that you are a different person in these different situations. People with BPD often report a large number of rather extreme life changes, as with the example of Wendy above, and they say that they don't have a very clear sense of who they are or where they are headed in life. This is another important part of identity disturbance—not having a defined sense of your core identity, or who you are as a person.

## Chronic Feelings of Emptiness

Another form that identity or self dysregulation can take is feeling empty much of the time. Some people with BPD say that they feel as if there is a void inside of them—like they are an empty shell. They may feel as if there's something missing, or as if there is a big hole that needs to be filled. This feeling is uncomfortable, frequent, and lasts for a long time (several hours to several days). Some people with BPD say that they feel as if they are "nothing" or "nobody," or as if they do not exist.

## *Cognitive Dysregulation*

*Another problem Wendy often struggled with was that of negative thoughts and a feeling of being spaced out when she was stressed. When she was upset, she sometimes did things that she didn't remember later on; sometimes she felt as if she were not inside her body. At other times, she felt as if she couldn't trust anyone, or she thought that people were trying to harm her or take advantage of her.*

With *cognitive dysregulation* a person experiences negative thinking and/or a disconnection from self or reality when he or she is very stressed out. It is important to note here that these types of problems are not always there and occur mainly when people with BPD are under a lot of stress or are really upset.

## Suspicious Thoughts or Dissociation When Experiencing Stress

One problem in this area involves suspicious, negative, or "paranoid" thinking about others' motives. If you struggle with this problem, it does not mean that you are delusional, schizophrenic, or psychotic. It means that when you are stressed out you start to become especially suspicious or worried about how others feel about you. You might start to believe that people are trying to be mean to you, take advantage of you, or harm you in some way. You might also think that people are looking at you and thinking negative or judgmental thoughts about you (such as "He's fat," "She's ugly," "I don't like her"). These experiences tend to happen when you are under stress or are feeling upset, but they don't happen very often when things are going smoothly.

The other aspect of cognitive dysregulation is dissociation. *Dissociation* is the experience of being checked out, spaced out, in a foggy mental state, not aware of your surroundings, or feeling as if you are not inside your body. Some people describe feeling as if they are floating to the ceiling and looking down on their body and the people around them. When present in BPD, dissociation occurs under stress.

Dissociation can actually be a way to escape distress. If your boss fires you, and you feel afraid, anxious, and angry, you might check out mentally for a little while in order to get away from your problems or your distress. The problem with dissociating, of course, is that it doesn't solve anything, and you may do things when you are dissociating that are dangerous (such as suicide attempts) or that you do not remember afterward (for example, risky one-night stands).

## *Not Everyone with BPD Is Alike*

As you may have noticed while reading this section and examining table 1.1, the "recipe" for BPD includes nine ingredients. In order to meet criteria for the diagnosis, you have to have at least five of these nine symptoms. You might be thinking, "Doesn't that mean that there are hundreds of different combinations of these nine symptoms, and they all would be called BPD?" And you would be correct. There are 151 different ways to meet criteria for a diagnosis of BPD. This means that not everyone who has the disorder is exactly alike.

Imagine that there was a diagnosis called "businessperson." (We don't have anything against businesspeople; we just think this is a good example!) When you think of a businessperson, you might think that he or she (1) wears expensive suits, (2) thinks about money, (3) works in a large office with a fancy desk, (4) has meetings with rich people, (5) sells things, (6) works long hours, (7) does a lot of paperwork, (8) is successful, and (9) gets up early to go to work.

If it only takes five of these features to be labeled a "businessperson," then two businesspeople might be quite different from one another. Sally, for example, never wears suits, works short hours, and gets up late, but she thinks about money all the time, is successful, sells lots of products, works in a large office with a fancy desk, and meets with rich people every Tuesday.

Ted, in contrast, always wears expensive suits, works long hours (sometimes sixty to seventy hours a week), does lots of paperwork, gets up before dawn to go to work, and meets with rich people five times per week. Unfortunately, Ted is completely and utterly unsuccessful despite his long hours. He also never thinks of money, can't sell anything to save his life, and works in a broom closet. Just as Sally and Ted are very different "businesspeople," two people who have the diagnosis of BPD might also be very different from one another.

# How Do You Figure Out Whether You Have BPD?

As we discussed above, the best way to determine whether you have BPD is to meet with a professional who is qualified to make diagnoses. Several different types of mental health professionals make diagnoses, including psychiatrists and psychologists. Psychiatrists are medical doctors with specialized training in medication-based and psychological treatments. Psychologists have Ph.D.'s (or Psy.D.s) in clinical or counseling psychology and have extensive training in psychological assessment and treatment. Both psychiatrists and psychologists are often in a good position to conduct a thorough assessment and make a diagnosis. Other people who make diagnoses include social workers, people with master's degrees in psychology, or people with Ph.D.'s or master's degrees in counseling psychology.

We recommend that you seek a professional with training and experience with personality disorders, and that you get a thorough assessment. Because BPD involves a long-standing pattern of relating to the world (and is something that many people have struggled with throughout their lives), the process of diagnosing BPD may take some time. Although it can be hard to be patient when you really want to find out what is wrong with you, a valid diagnosis is important, and it may require several appointments and a lot of talking. It is also important that the professional you work with understands how to distinguish BPD from other disorders that might look like BPD, such as bipolar disorder or major depression. In chapter 7, we discuss in more detail the ways in which you might seek assessment and treatment for issues related to BPD.

## Summary

Below is a brief summary of what we have covered in this chapter. We hope that you find the information in this chapter to be helpful as you continue to explore this book and learn more about BPD.

- BPD is a personality disorder that involves instability in several areas of life.
- People with BPD struggle with their emotions, identity, relationships, behavior, and thinking.
- Not all people with BPD are exactly alike.

- Having BPD doesn't mean that you are sick, unlikable, flawed, or have some kind of illness or a bad personality.
- Seek help and get a thorough assessment from a trained professional if you believe that you might have some of the features of BPD.

# 2

# Borderline Personality Disorder: Is What They Say Really True?

One thing that researchers, clinicians, and other health professionals have always agreed on is that having information is essential to the recovery process, regardless of what problems you struggle with. For medical and psychological disorders alike, it is very helpful to have accurate information regarding the causes, symptoms, and progression of the disorder. If you were visiting some friends in Los Angeles but didn't know their address or even the street they lived on, your trip would be confusing, stressful, and overwhelming. Knowing that you're going to Los Angeles is a good first step, but it doesn't help you find your friends once you get there. Likewise, if you are struggling with BPD or other problems, just knowing that you have these problems is a good starting point. However, having more specific information can give you a clearer sense of what is going on with your body, mind, relationships, and life in general. With this knowledge comes a better idea of how to address the problems you may be having. In this way, simply knowing the facts about a disorder may be one of the most important first steps in recovering from that disorder. And, as you will see throughout this book, we now know a lot about what causes BPD and what to expect if you suffer from this disorder.

Unfortunately, though, accurate information is not always readily available. Instead, misinformation abounds, and it can be very difficult to sort out the fact from the fiction, and the truth from the myths. This can make the journey to recovery much more difficult. Imagine that you had embarked upon your trip to Los Angeles with a trusty map in hand, but it turned out that it wasn't a map of Los Angeles—it was a map of Boston! Or, what if your friends were new to the area and mistakenly gave you the wrong directions to their house. In either case, your trip would be very confusing, and you would probably get lost. So it's not enough to have just any information—it has to be accurate information. And, unfortunately, it seems that despite all the new information we are learning about this disorder, persistent myths about BPD continue to lead people astray and add to the stigma associated with this disorder. In this chapter, we review and challenge some common myths and misconceptions about BPD.

# Stigma and Borderline Personality Disorder

Although many mental health problems have a social stigma attached to them, the stigma associated with BPD is especially strong. Advocacy groups and consumer organizations like the National Alliance on Mental Illness (NAMI) have worked tirelessly over the past decade to decrease the stigma attached to severe mental illness. As a result, we now see fewer negative portrayals of people with these mental illnesses in the media, as well as less misinformation in general. However, the stigma associated with BPD seems to persist to this day.

Why would society stigmatize people with BPD more than people with other disorders? Although we don't know for sure, there are a few possible reasons. First, until recently, the causes of BPD were poorly understood, and, unfortunately, sometimes people react most negatively to problems they can't understand. Second, as we mentioned earlier, many of the symptoms of BPD hit a nerve for people in our society. Some of the behaviors that go along with BPD may be shocking and difficult to understand. For example, self-harm and suicide attempts may frighten and confuse others, and they can be hard to relate to. When people don't understand a behavior, and especially when that behavior scares them, it is sometimes easier to judge the person who is engaging in that behavior than it is to make an effort to understand that person. Also, our society generally values being calm, cool, collected, and in control—something that people with BPD often struggle with. Indeed, because people with BPD have very strong emotions and often express these emotions in extreme or dramatic ways, people who value being in control of emotions may judge people with BPD, and they may even develop inaccurate or negative beliefs about people with BPD. The intense emotions and shocking or frightening behaviors seen in BPD may form the basis of social stigma about BPD.

Finally, another source of stigma may be the television and film media. The media seem to be drawn to BPD—probably because of some of the strengths that often go along with BPD. People with BPD can be dramatic, exciting, and charismatic, and the intensity of their experiences can be engaging. So it is probably not surprising that television and film producers are interested in depicting such strong, intense, and dramatic characters. The problem is that in seeking to get good ratings and go for the dramatic effect, the media tend to depict one-sided and simplistic representations of BPD that are usually negative. In fact, negative, inaccurate, and insensitive portrayals of people with BPD are seen quite regularly. Although it is likely not done with a malicious intent, these portrayals contribute to the stigma attached to BPD and make it harder for the public to really understand this disorder.

## Common Myths About Borderline Personality Disorder

Given the continued myths and misinformation about BPD, as well as the negative and inaccurate portrayals of BPD in the media, we believe it is important to clear up some of the most common and problematic myths about BPD. Therefore, what follows is a list of the seven most common and pervasive myths about BPD and the people who suffer from it, as well as the facts about this disorder that counter these myths.

## Myth 1: People with BPD Are Manipulative and Attention Seeking

This is one of the most common myths about BPD. In fact, this myth is so common that it is found not only in the media but also in some academic clinical and research literature. This myth likely developed as a misguided attempt to explain some of the problems that people with BPD tend to struggle with, especially suicidal and self-harm behaviors. As we mentioned before, for people who have not struggled with these behaviors, seeing someone engage in them can be shocking, scary, and incomprehensible. As a result, suicidal and self-harm behaviors can evoke intense emotional responses in others, including fear, anger, sadness, guilt, and confusion. What's more, because these behaviors are so serious and life threatening, many people find that they want to intervene quickly to help or support the person who engages in them.

We believe that this very common desire to help people with serious and life-threatening problems may have ironically led to the belief that people with BPD are manipulative. Specifically, seeing themselves act quickly to provide help, support, and reassurance to people with BPD, some mental health professionals may have concluded that people with BPD are using self-harm or suicide attempts to manipulate others into paying attention to them or helping them. The problem with this way of thinking is that you can't infer a person's intentions based on the effects of her or his behavior. For example, let's say that you were rushing to work in order to avoid being late, and you ran a red light and struck a pedestrian. Saying that people with BPD attempt suicide in order to manipulate others into providing support is like saying that you ran the red light in order to hit the pedestrian. In another example, if we saw a woman drink a huge glass of water, we may assume that she was drinking that water because she was thirsty. But there are other reasons why someone might drink water that we might not be taking into account. For example, maybe the woman wasn't thirsty but had a scratchy throat. Maybe she was trying to stop herself from hiccupping. Maybe she was hungry. The point is, there is really no way of knowing and, if we simply assume, we may come to the wrong conclusion. The same principle applies here. Knowing that self-harm and suicide attempts may lead others to provide attention or help does not actually tell us *why* someone engages in those behaviors. In fact, as we discuss in chapter 6, research clearly indicates that influencing others is not the primary reason people hurt themselves or try to kill themselves.

What's more, even if people have learned that the only way to get any kind of attention from someone else is to engage in a behavior as extreme as self-harm, the fact that they resort to this behavior does not mean that they are manipulative. It may simply mean that they are desperately in need of some kind of attention from another human being, and they have not yet learned any other way of getting that need met. In fact, attention and regard from others is a basic human need. Of course, we all would rather get positive attention than negative attention; however, in some cases, that positive attention is not available. In these cases, people are generally willing to accept negative attention rather than no attention at all. So, the assumption that someone who engages in self-harm or attempts suicide in order to get some needed care or attention is "manipulative" overlooks the basic human need involved in this situation.

The message to remember here is that people with BPD are not manipulative. The behaviors that often go along with BPD serve an important purpose for that person, even if the purpose is not readily seen by an outside observer.

## *Myth 2: People with BPD Are Violent Individuals, at High Risk for Harming Others*

This is simply not true. Despite the way BPD is often portrayed on the big and small screens, people with BPD are not generally violent and are actually at very low risk of hurting others. In fact, many people with BPD will go to great lengths to avoid hurting others in any way at all, sacrificing their own needs and wants to try to make others happy. People with BPD are often scared of being alone and desperately want to hold onto their relationships; therefore, they often go out of their way to take care of others. They certainly wouldn't want to do anything that might cause someone to leave or reject them.

Most researchers would agree that people with BPD are far more likely to hurt themselves than to hurt other people. One of the hallmark symptoms of BPD is self-destructive and self-damaging behaviors, and the general consensus is that people with BPD tend to direct anger inward rather than outward. In our experience, people with BPD are much more likely to feel anger toward themselves than toward others, and they are much more likely to harm themselves as well. Indeed, one of the primary factors thought to distinguish BPD from another personality disorder, *antisocial personality disorder* (ASPD), is the extent to which anger and harm are directed inward versus outward. Specifically, BPD is thought to involve internalized anger and the risk for self-harm, and ASPD is thought to involve anger expressed toward other people and a greater risk for violence toward others.

Finally, it is important to note that many people with BPD are actually scared of the expression of anger and try to avoid experiencing or expressing anger at all costs. In some cases, this is due to a history of severe childhood abuse, including extensive physical abuse. As a result of their own experiences with extreme abuse and firsthand knowledge of how terrible and devastating it is, some people with BPD develop a no-tolerance policy regarding any form of anger or physical aggression and decide never to inflict such harm on others. One way that some people with BPD shut the door on aggression toward others is to stifle any expression of anger. Although the fear and avoidance of any level of anger has its own downside (like making it hard to stand up for yourself or deal with the life problems that lead to anger), it does help debunk the myth that people with BPD are especially violent.

## *Myth 3: BPD Is a Life Sentence*

Until several years ago, people thought that BPD was incurable, and that once you had this disorder you were stuck with it for life. (This is one reason why some clinicians actually refused to diagnose patients with BPD—they feared that patients would be burdened with this diagnosis and judged as untreatable.) We now know that this is not true, and that BPD actually has a very good prognosis. In fact, recent research suggests that people are more likely to recover from BPD than from bipolar disorder (Lieb, Zanarini, et al. 2004). This is likely due to our increased knowledge about BPD, as well as improvements in treatments for this disorder. We will talk more about the current knowledge about the progression of BPD in chapter 4, summarizing recent research on how long it takes most people to recover from BPD. For now, though, the important thing to remember is that there is plenty of hope for people diagnosed with BPD, as most people recover from this disorder and go on to develop the lives that they want to live.

## Myth 4: BPD Is Untreatable

This myth is related to the preceding myth and is an interesting one because of why it may have developed. Before we had the knowledge we now have about BPD, many mental health professionals had difficulties treating people with BPD and saw that their treatments did not seem to be working. Therefore, they decided that BPD must not be a treatable disorder. How about that? This is like going to the gym, trying in vain to lift a 200-pound weight, and then concluding that 200-pound weights cannot be lifted. A similar sequence of events happened with regard to treatments for BPD. From what we know now, previous treatments for BPD were just not effective (Lieb,

Zanarini, et al. 2004). They were not specialized, nor were they based on a good understanding of the causes of BPD; thus, they simply didn't work—at no fault of the client or the disorder. The fact that these earlier treatments did not work, however, does not mean that BPD cannot be treated. In fact, we now know that people with BPD can make incredible progress in relatively short periods of time when treated with therapies developed specifically for BPD (Bateman and Fonagy 1999; Linehan 1993a).

Specifically, we now have a lot of evidence to indicate that a variety of types of treatments (whether they are cognitive, behavioral, or psychoanalytic in focus) are effective in treating BPD (Lieb, Zanarini, et al. 2004). These treatments can dramatically reduce the likelihood of suicide attempts and self-harm, as well as depression and anxiety, all in just a year or so (Bateman and Fonagy 1999; Linehan 1993a). What's more, even treatments three months in length have been found to help people with BPD, reducing mood symptoms and self-harm, and improving overall everyday functioning (Gratz, Lacroce, and Gunderson 2006; Gunderson et al. 2005).

## Myth 5: BPD Is Caused by Bad Parents

Many mental health professionals used to think that BPD was caused by the patient's bad relationship with her or his mother during early childhood. In fact, there was a tendency throughout the fields of psychology and psychiatry to blame mothers for many problems experienced by children. Although this "bad mothering" fallacy has been corrected in many areas of psychology, the belief that BPD is caused by abusive, neglectful, or bad parenting still exists.

There are a couple of things to keep in mind about this myth. First, there is a difference between something that increases the risk for a disorder (a "risk factor") and something that is necessary for this disorder to develop (a "necessary cause"). With BPD, there is evidence that childhood abuse increases the risk for BPD and may contribute to the development of the disorder for some people. However, not everyone with BPD has been abused. In fact, most people with BPD do not have a history of abuse. The same thing applies to neglect. Although we know that neglect increases the risk for BPD, and is one of the potential causes, not everyone who has BPD was neglected by their parents. Therefore, the experience of a bad relationship with one's caregivers is not necessary for the development of BPD. There are many other factors that lead to BPD that don't have anything to do with abuse (we'll talk about these in chapter 3).

What we know is that BPD is caused by a combination of personality traits and stressful experiences growing up. The thing is, those stressful experiences range from severe physical or sexual abuse to a poor fit between the person and her or his family. For example, one factor that may lead to BPD is the feeling that you are different from everyone around you—for example, if you are very emotional and the rest of your family members are more reserved. Growing up in a family where everyone seems different from you can be really stressful. You might start to feel like you are the black sheep or an outsider and believe that something is wrong with you. Other people in your family may not understand you, or may see things differently. You may even come to believe that you are somehow wrong for being so different. When combined with certain personality traits, a stressor like this can lead to BPD.

Similarly, even if parents are not around as much as they would like, or as available to their children as they might wish, this does not mean that these parents are bad or neglectful. In fact, many parents these days are finding that they do not have as much time to spend with their children as they would like. Some families don't get to spend a lot of time with one another because they are struggling to make ends meet, or they are so busy that there is not enough time in the day to do everything that needs to be done. This by itself will not necessarily lead to BPD, and in most cases it doesn't. But if someone who possesses certain personality traits or has undergone other stressful experiences (for example, with peers) finds herself or himself in a situation like this, it could lead to BPD—not because the parents are bad, but because the specific needs of that particular child were not met in that family.

Therefore, although being abused or neglected as a child is definitely one of the things that may cause BPD, not everyone who develops BPD has had these experiences. Indeed, in many cases, the family members of people with BPD work incredibly hard to help that person in any way they can. These families are doing the best they can to help a loved one who just happened to be born more sensitive and emotional than some other people.

## Myth 6: People with BPD Are Crazy and Irrational

This myth couldn't be farther from the truth. People with BPD are in a lot of pain, and they struggle with intense, overwhelming emotions. At times, this struggle may get the better of them, and lead them to do or say things in a desperate attempt to make themselves feel better. Although they will often regret these things later on, in the moment these actions provide much-needed relief from intense emotional pain.

As mentioned previously, we know that all behaviors have a purpose and meet some important need for that individual (even if they also cause that person further problems and distress in the long run). Even behaviors that may seem incomprehensible to someone who has not struggled with them (such as suicide attempts, self-harm, and drug abuse) serve an important purpose for that person in that moment. In fact, people often attempt suicide, use drugs, or harm themselves in order to meet some very basic human needs—for example, to feel better, get some relief, or release emotional pain. These behaviors are really neither crazy nor irrational. Indeed, they often work very well to meet these needs in the short run. The problem is that these self-destructive behaviors have serious downsides over the long term.

It is also important to keep in mind that people with BPD are not inherently different from other people; it's not as if they are from another planet, or made up of a different substance than everyone else is! In fact, the personality traits of people with BPD are traits that everyone has, to a greater or lesser extent. One of the personality traits related to BPD is *neuroticism,* which basically means "negative emotions." We all experience negative emotions to some extent. People with BPD just seem to experience stronger negative emotions than some other people do.

It's also important to keep in mind that some of the personality traits found among people with BPD can actually be strengths. For example, research has shown that people with BPD tend to experience their emotions more intensely than other people do (Henry et al. 2001; Koenigsberg et al. 2002). Now, the downside here is that negative, uncomfortable emotions (such as sadness, guilt, shame) are experienced more strongly; however, the upside is that positive emotions (such as excitement, happiness, joy) are also experienced more intensely. Having intense emotions can be a plus in that it can make our lives feel fuller, richer, and more exciting.

Finally, although some of the thoughts that people with BPD have may appear irrational to others, they are in fact quite understandable and reasonable. People with BPD often have thoughts and fears that others will reject or abandon them. They may also feel as if others are out to get them or deliberately cause them harm. While these thoughts and evaluations may not be accurate in the present, they may have been at one time. That is, thoughts don't just pop up out of the blue. How we think, how we evaluate situations or others' behaviors, and how we view ourselves originate from our life experiences. Many people with BPD have been in situations where actual abandonment or rejection did occur. As a result, it is only natural that they might expect this behavior from other people. These expectations are our body's natural way of preparing itself for (and protecting itself from) some negative outcome. Viewing these thoughts as irrational dismisses the fact that they are based on people's experiences, and it fails to acknowledge the life experiences often associated with this disorder (such as abuse, neglect, rejection, and so on). In fact, the thoughts of people with BPD are very understandable when you begin to consider where they come from.

## Myth 7: BPD Is Only Found in Women

At a basic level, this idea is simply not true. Men can and do develop BPD. In fact, research suggests that men with BPD have the same problems and struggles as women with BPD do, and that the disorder looks the same in people of both genders.

Nevertheless, although we know that men can have BPD, it is also the case that BPD is diagnosed much more often in women than in men—about three times as often in fact (Gunderson 2001). We don't know why this is the case; however, there are a couple of reasons why women may be diagnosed with BPD more than men.

One possible explanation is related to the way boys and girls are raised. Because children are taught that being emotional, expressing feelings, and relying on relationships are characteristics of girls, boys may express their emotions or react to their distress in ways that are different from those associated with BPD, resulting in a different diagnosis. For example, rather than crying, males may behave aggressively. Rather than seeking out a relationship to feel less alone, males may turn to drugs to numb their pain. Conversely, since many of the characteristics of BPD are variants of stereotypical "female" characteristics, girls may learn it is okay to express and act on their emotional pain in those ways.

Another possible explanation is that clinicians are more likely to diagnose women with BPD and men with other disorders (like ASPD) simply because of gender-role stereotypes. Because clinicians think that BPD is more common among women, they may notice it more often in women and fail to notice it in men. Similarly, because

BPD has certain features that are more acceptable in our society in women than in men (for example, being emotional, relying on relationships), clinicians may believe that this is a disorder restricted to women, and they may overlook it or disregard it in men.

## Summary

In this chapter, we challenged and debunked some common myths and misperceptions about BPD. Of course, this is not an exhaustive list and there are likely many more myths out there; however, the ones we presented seem to be some of the most common and important myths surrounding this disorder currently. The research on BPD is growing every day, and we have a much better understanding of this disorder today than we did even five to ten years ago. Unfortunately, though, despite this better understanding, many of these myths continue to persist and increase the level of stigma attached to BPD. Probably one of the most important things to remember in thinking about BPD is that this is a very human disorder. At its core is not maliciousness, craziness, irrationality, or disregard for others. Instead, BPD is a disorder that stems largely from understandable (though sometimes misguided) attempts to meet basic human needs. Only by continuing to debunk myths about this disorder and learning about its true causes and characteristics will we improve society's perceptions of BPD and increase our understanding of how best to help people who struggle with this disorder.

## Table 2.1 Seven Common Myths About BPD

1. People with BPD are manipulative and attention seeking.
2. People with BPD are violent individuals, at high risk for harming others.
3. BPD is a life sentence.
4. BPD is untreatable.
5. BPD is caused by bad parents.
6. People with BPD are crazy and irrational.
7. BPD is only found in women.

# 3

# What Causes Borderline Personality Disorder?

In this chapter, we go through what we know so far about the causes of borderline personality disorder (BPD). Keep in mind that nobody is 100 percent certain about what causes BPD. But findings from many studies over the last several years have suggested that BPD results from a combination of genetics, biology, personality traits, and stressful experiences.

## Can You Inherit Borderline Personality Disorder?

*Casey's family had always been just a little different from other families. They reacted really strongly to very small things. They were always upset or stressed out about something, and they argued all the time. Casey sometimes saw scars or marks on his mother's arm, but he never quite knew what they were. His parents always seemed to be on some kind of roller-coaster ride—fighting one minute, and then saying loving things to each other the next minute. Only when he went to therapy did he realize that his parents had many of the same problems that he had.*

One important question that you might have is whether you can inherit BPD from your parents. One way researchers have tried to answer this question is by conducting studies with twins. Basically, researchers have taken several sets of twins and looked to see whether identical twins are more likely to share a disorder than fraternal twins are. As you may know, identical twins come from the same ovum (or egg) and share 100 percent of their genes. In contrast, fraternal twins come from different ova and share only 50 percent of their genes. So, if identical twins are more likely to share BPD than fraternal twins, then BPD is more likely to be *heritable* (able to be inherited).

There have only been a few small twin studies on BPD, and the findings are mixed. The largest study (done in Norway) found that, if you have BPD, the chances that your *identical* twin has BPD are 35 percent, but the chances that your *fraternal* twin has BPD are around 7 percent (Torgersen et al. 2000). These findings suggest that BPD can be inherited (at least partially). Some research has indicated that BPD may be about 50 percent heritable (Torgersen 2005).

Another way to examine whether you can inherit BPD is to look at the rates of BPD among *first-degree relatives* (parents and siblings) of people with BPD. The idea here is that if BPD is heritable, and you have BPD, then your parents and siblings might be likely to have BPD themselves. Findings from a few studies have indicated that between 10 and 20 percent of first-degree relatives of people with BPD also have BPD (Baron, Gruen, and Asnis 1985; Links, Steiner, and Huxley 1988; Zanarini et al. 1988). This sounds quite low, right? If the disorder were very heritable, you might expect most first-degree relatives to have it. But think about the overall prevalence rate of BPD—it's around 1.6 percent. So, this means that first-degree relatives of people with BPD are over twelve times more likely to have BPD than are people in the general population.

## *What About Genes?*

Assuming that BPD is around 50 percent heritable, you might be wondering exactly what kinds of genes you've inherited if you have BPD. Now, this is a very complicated question, and there's no clear answer right now. Making it more complex is the fact that the activity of your genes can ultimately influence the environment (by influencing your behavior), and the environment can influence the activities of your genes. The current thinking is that people's genes make them more vulnerable and sensitive to stress in the environment. To put it another way, genes don't cause BPD on their own, but certain genes or combinations of genes might make you more vulnerable to developing BPD if you are exposed to stress in your environment. Also, no single gene can be considered the primary cause of BPD. In most cases, many different genes work together to influence whether a person has a psychiatric disorder.

To our knowledge, there have been no published studies on specific genes related to BPD. But with all of the progress that has come from the mapping of the human genome, it is likely that these studies will start popping up very soon. Right now, the best we can do is look at research on the genes that are involved in personality traits that go along with BPD.

## Personality Traits, Genes, and BPD

*Casey was always an emotional and impulsive person. In fact, many people liked him for these very qualities—he was popular in high school. He was willing to take risks that other people refused to take, and he was the ringleader when he and his friends went bungee jumping or cliff diving. Casey always seemed to be able to get his hands on drugs and alcohol as well. He was also a very sensitive person, easily hurt by the mildest criticism. His moods were very strong; whether he was angry, happy, sad, or anxious, he felt these emotions strongly and vividly.*

Because BPD is a personality disorder, you might be wondering what kinds of personality characteristics or traits are related to BPD. So, what exactly are *personality traits?* Personality traits are ways of thinking, feeling, and behaving that remain pretty much the same across different situations throughout your life. They are the elements of who you are as a person. When someone says, "She's a real character!" or "He loves to socialize with other people" or "He's an introvert," they are really talking about personality traits.

**Impulsivity and dopamine genes.** One personality trait related to BPD is *impulsivity,* the tendency to act quickly, on the spur of the moment, without thinking things through (Schalling 1978). If you have BPD, you may have noticed that you tend to be on the impulsive side. Maybe you make very quick decisions without considering what might happen as a result. For instance, you might choose to go home with someone you have just met, without thinking about the fact that you could get hurt. Or, you might decide on a whim to binge on food or use drugs without thinking about all of the negative consequences. Impulsivity is a feature of BPD that can get you into trouble and cause you distress.

Indeed, people with BPD tend to be more impulsive than people without BPD and people with other personality disorders (Morey et al. 2002). People with BPD also have higher rates of other personality traits that are similar to impulsivity, such as *novelty seeking* (the tendency to seek out interesting or novel situations) (Ball et al. 1997). In addition, impulsivity is related to suicide attempts among people with BPD. The higher your impulsivity is, the more likely you are to have attempted suicide in the past (Brodsky, Malone, and Ellis 1997).

Findings from some studies have suggested that people with a certain type of the DRD4 gene may have lower *dopamine* activity and are likely to have characteristics related to impulsivity, such as novelty seeking (Ebstein et al. 1996). Dopamine is a chemical in your brain involved in your mood, your experience of pleasure, and the regulation of body movement. Of course, this dopamine gene does not explain all occurrences of impulsive behavior, and the findings so far have been mixed (Strobel et al. 2003). Some studies have found a connection between DRD4 and personality, and others have not, and no studies so far have looked at DRD4 in relation to BPD. Future research on the DRD4 gene might help us to better understand impulsivity and BPD.

**Negative emotions and serotonin genes.** Another set of personality traits related to BPD involves vulnerability to negative emotions. One of these traits is called *neuroticism,* which is basically the tendency to experience negative emotions. If you have a high level of neuroticism, you probably experience many negative emotions on a regular basis. This, of course, is one of the features of BPD (see chapter 2), so if you have BPD you are probably no stranger to negative emotions!

We all experience negative emotions sometimes and we all have some amount of neuroticism. It's just that some people are more neurotic than others. Research tells us that people with BPD tend to receive higher scores on evaluations for neuroticism than people without BPD (Farmer and Nelson-Gray 1995). People with BPD also score higher on evaluations for personality traits related to neuroticism such as *harm avoidance* (the tendency to avoid risky or potentially harmful activities) (Ball et al. 1997) and *anxiety* (Farmer and Nelson-Gray 1995). Now, this probably isn't that surprising. You know by now that people with BPD are very emotional. And there's nothing wrong with experiencing strong, negative emotions. It's what you do with those emotions that's most important.

Some researchers have looked into neuroticism to see what genes are related to this personality trait. Some people think that the brain chemical *serotonin* may be related to negative emotions, depression, anxiety, and neuroticism. Serotonin is a neurotransmitter that controls mood, hunger, temperature, sexual activity, sleep, and aggression, among other things. Some studies have shown that people who rate high in neuroticism are likely to have a certain form of a gene that is related to low levels of serotonin activity (compared with people who aren't neurotic or who don't have that form of the gene) (Lesch et al. 1996; Lesch and Heils 2000). So, having a certain form of this gene might make it more likely that people will have low serotonin activity and higher negative emotions (neuroticism). In turn, if you have high levels of negative emotions, you might be more likely to develop BPD.

# Borderline Personality Disorder and the Brain

*Casey told his therapist, "There's always been something weird about me. I don't react to things like other people do." He described how he felt like his brain just spun out of control whenever he got upset. He couldn't think clearly, he couldn't get himself calmed down, and he couldn't control what he did. It almost felt like there was someone else up there shifting the gears in his brain. He asked, "Is my brain different from other people's brains, or am I just crazy, or both?"*

If you have BPD, you might have wondered whether your brain is somehow different from the brains of people who don't have BPD. You might have noticed that you react differently to things than other people around you do. You might think differently, feel emotions more intensely, or have more trouble stopping yourself from engaging in impulsive actions. If so, you might have wondered whether you simply have a different kind of brain than other people do.

As it turns out, it is not as simple as that. The brain is very complex, with many different structures and systems that interact with each other in ways that scientists are just beginning to understand. Differences in your brain could have been there from birth or even before birth, or they could have developed over time. Many things can influence how the brain functions and even how large certain brain areas are. Brain differences between people who have BPD and those who don't have BPD could be due to genes; exposure to unhealthy conditions or substances during gestation (stressful events, drugs, medication, or alcohol use); stressful events during infancy, childhood, or later; alcohol use; drug use; or any number of other things that affect the brain.

Below, we will go through some of the brain areas that may be involved in BPD. These areas include the limbic system and the prefrontal cortex, as well as the hypothalamic-pituitary-adrenal axis.

## *The Limbic System and the Prefrontal Cortex*

The limbic system is an area of your brain that has to do with emotions, memory, and pleasure, among other things. Some of the brain structures in the limbic system include the *amygdala* and the *hippocampus.* The amygdala is basically the emotional center of your brain. When you experience an emotional event, your amygdala stands at attention and gets active. The hippocampus, in contrast, is involved in learning and memory.

As we have discussed, BPD is an emotional disorder. If you have BPD, you probably experience intense emotions that sometimes change quite rapidly and at other times stick around for an agonizingly long time. You may also have trouble bringing yourself down once you feel a strong emotion. So, it's probably not surprising that researchers have found differences in the amygdalas of people with BPD and people without BPD.

The research shows that, compared with those who do not have BPD, people with BPD have smaller amygdalas (Schmahl et al. 2003; Tebartz van Elst et al. 2003), and certain areas of their amygdalas are more reactive to emotional stimulation. For instance, one study monitored how the amygdala acted when people in the study were looking at faces with different types of emotional expressions (such as sadness, or anger). People with BPD had stronger activation in their left amygdalas (Herpertz et al. 2001).

Research has also shown that people with BPD tend to have a smaller hippocampus than people who do not have BPD (Schmahl et al. 2003; Tebartz van Elst et al. 2003). It is interesting to note that people with post-traumatic stress disorder (PTSD) also tend to have a smaller hippocampus, but that only among people with BPD are both the hippocampus and the amygdala smaller.

Another area of the brain that seems to be involved in BPD is the *prefrontal cortex,* a small but very complex area of the brain that is involved in many different functions. The prefrontal cortex is most well known because of the case of Phineas Gage in the 1800s. Phineas Gage was a railroad worker who was working one day clearing paths for new railroad tracks. In a tragic accident, a steel rod shot right through Mr. Gage's prefrontal cortex. Unbelievably, he survived and continued to live for many years with very few physical problems.

Unfortunately, however, he experienced some major personality changes. He became socially inappropriate, could not hold a job, made poor decisions, had angry outbursts, and was quite impulsive after his accident. This case sparked research on the prefrontal cortex and its important role in helping us control our behavior, make reasonable decisions, entertain different choices and select the most effective ones, and deal with our emotions (Damasio 1994).

In fact, there is some evidence that activity in the prefrontal cortex influences some of the activity in the limbic system (including the amygdala). Basically, it seems that activity in the prefrontal cortex can keep the activity in this emotional center of the brain in check. Indeed, some of the research on BPD has found that people with BPD experience lower activity in certain areas of the prefrontal cortex (such as the anterior cingulate cortex, among other regions) when they are exposed to stressful memories (Schmahl et al. 2003). If people with BPD have low levels of activity in the prefrontal cortex, then the prefrontal cortex may not be active enough in certain ways to curb the activity of the amygdala. As a result, when they experience a stressful event, their emotions might spin out of control.

## *The Hypothalamic-Pituitary-Adrenal Axis*

The hypothalamic-pituitary-adrenal axis, or HPA axis, is another area of the brain related to BPD. Two of the brain structures within the HPA axis are the *hypothalamus* and the *pituitary gland.* Both of these areas influence your body's response to stress, and higher activity in the HPA axis leads to greater concentrations in your system of a stress hormone called *cortisol.* When researchers study the HPA axis, they often get people to provide saliva samples to see how much cortisol is in their systems. This is an indirect measure of how active your HPA axis is. The more active it is, generally, the more cortisol is in your system. So, an overly active (or hyperactive) HPA axis means that you have a hyperactive biological stress response.

If you have BPD, you might have noticed that stressors that seem minor to other people sometimes throw you over the edge. You might go through periods when you feel extremely tense, and find yourself getting irritated at even the smallest things, like your computer not working properly, forgetting to put out the garbage before the garbage truck arrives, losing your keys, receiving criticism from your boss at work, spilling your coffee, or any of the other daily hassles and stresses that we all go through on a regular basis. In other words, you might find that, sometimes, you have an exaggerated stress response.

Some research on the HPA axis has found that people with BPD demonstrate cortisol responses that are exaggerated compared to people who do not have BPD (Grossman, Yehuda, and Siever 1997; Lieb, Rexhausen, et al. 2004). Other studies have found that hyperactivity in the HPA axis might predispose people to attempt suicide (van Heeringen et al. 2000).

Another important thing to know is that stressful and traumatic life events can increase your likelihood of having an exaggerated cortisol response and hyperactivity in the HPA axis (Carrion et al. 2002; Essex et al. 2002). It makes sense, doesn't it? If you are severely hurt or traumatized, your body might decide, "Hey, it's time to prepare my system just in case this happens again." The cortisol response is part of your body's response to stress.

So, through experiencing very stressful events, your body might start becoming too reactive for its own good. As we mentioned above, you might feel extremely stressed out about even relatively minor things (like spilling your coffee). This kind of reaction happens to all of us from time to time—we can think of many times when we got more stressed out than we wanted to while driving, after spilling something, or when a computer or photocopier doesn't work properly. But if you have BPD this might happen to you even more strongly or more often. And this might be partly due to the biological effects of past stressful experiences in your life.

## Adverse Life Events: Borderline Personality Disorder and the Environment

*Casey could not seem to get his life under control. It seemed that he was always in the middle of some kind of breakup, getting fired from his job, getting into car accidents, and so on. Although he was not abused as a child sexually or physically, he did remember that his parents ignored him or got really angry whenever he got upset. When his uncle died and he couldn't stop crying, they were nice to him at first, but then they kept telling him to get over it. Eventually they yelled at him whenever he seemed sad about it.*

As we have discussed, BPD is a complex disorder, and the causes of BPD are just as complex. Many different things have to come together for someone to have BPD. In addition to genes, the brain, and personality, certain life experiences may cause BPD. BPD is not just about how you were born, but also about your life experiences.

## *Nature and Nurture*

You have probably heard of the "nature versus nurture" debate, which has to do with whether psychiatric disorders are related to hardwired genetic factors that are present when we are born ("nature"), or whether they are related to the environment ("nurture"). Frankly, this debate is outdated. The research says that both nature and nurture play a role in all psychiatric disorders. What's more, we now know that it's not even possible to separate nature from nurture—the latest research indicates that the environment can influence the activity of a person's genes (Johnson and Edwards 2002). The environment can also influence the activity of your brain, the size of certain areas of your brain, and the biological systems of your body. Keep this idea in mind as you read on about the environmental causes that interact with your genes, your brain, and your body to produce BPD.

## *Traumatic Experiences and Childhood Maltreatment*

The environmental factor in BPD that is discussed most often is childhood maltreatment. *Childhood maltreatment* is exactly what it sounds like: being mistreated; being neglected; being physically, emotionally, or sexually abused; or not receiving enough support when growing up. In particular, many studies have indicated a link between BPD and childhood sexual abuse. Although the findings vary from one study to another, the best guess is that about half of people with BPD have had some kind of childhood sexual abuse (Silk, Wolf, and Ben-Ami 2005).

Could childhood sexual abuse be one possible cause of BPD? It is quite likely that childhood sexual abuse, especially by someone who is supposed to be caring for the child (such as a parent, childcare provider, or relative), could definitely put someone at risk for some of the problems that go along with BPD. Some studies have shown that more severe abuse is related to more severe cognitive and interpersonal symptoms of BPD (Zanarini et al. 2002).

Cognitive symptoms of BPD include dissociating ("checking out"). Dissociation is a common experience among people who have undergone traumatic events. Although it can eventually become a problem for those experiencing it, we believe that the reason people may start to dissociate in the first place is because dissociating can give them relief from stress and emotional turmoil, which for some people is related to past abuse.

Suspiciousness (difficulty trusting others, or thinking that others are viewing one in a negative way) is another cognitive symptom of BPD. If you were sexually abused as a child, it wouldn't be surprising if you had difficulty trusting people and had suspicious thoughts from time to time. In fact, being a little suspicious and careful about whom you trust might even protect you at times.

The interpersonal symptoms that seem to be related to abuse involve, for the most part, fears of abandonment; efforts to avoid abandonment; and rocky, chaotic relationships. Being abused as a child can make it very difficult to feel secure in your relationships with other people, especially if the person who abused you was your mother, father, or caregiver.

Suicidal and self-harm behaviors also seem to be related to sexual abuse. Perhaps not surprisingly, some research has found that more severe sexual abuse is related to more severe suicidal and self-harm behavior among people with BPD (Silk et al. 1995; Zanarini et al. 2002).

Overall, then, there is some evidence that childhood sexual abuse is connected with some of the problems that are typical of BPD. However, as Dr. Mary Zanarini has stated, "childhood sexual abuse is neither necessary nor sufficient for the development of borderline personality disorder" (Zanarini et al. 1997, 1105). The best conclusion we can make is that childhood abuse (especially sexual abuse) is related to *some* of the problems of *some* people who have BPD.

## Is BPD a Form of Post-traumatic Stress Disorder?

Because of this link between abuse and BPD, some people actually think that BPD is a complicated form of *post-traumatic stress disorder* (PTSD). As we mention in the next chapter, PTSD is a disorder that can develop after someone experiences a horrifying, frightening, or extremely traumatic event. If you have PTSD, you might repeatedly experience thoughts, memories, images, or dreams of the traumatic event. You might even have *flashbacks*—vivid images of the trauma that come to mind unexpectedly and make you feel like the event is happening all over again. Sexual abuse is one type of traumatic experience that might lead to PTSD.

We don't believe that BPD is a form of PTSD, however, for a couple of reasons. First, around 50 percent of people with BPD do not report childhood sexual abuse, and up to 54 percent of them do not meet criteria for PTSD

(Lieb, Zanarini, et al. 2004). Second, some people with BPD don't report having experienced any kind of traumatic event. In order to receive a diagnosis of PTSD, you need to have experienced a severely stressful experience. If you haven't had a traumatic experience, you can't have PTSD. As we discuss in chapter 5, BPD and PTSD sometimes do go hand in hand and can be caused by the same experiences; however, not everyone with BPD has PTSD. Thus, we do not think that BPD is a form of complicated PTSD. PTSD seems to be a separate disorder altogether, although trauma certainly plays a role in BPD for some people.

## *Invalidating Environments*

Besides actual abuse, other childhood experiences also can lead to BPD. One of these experiences is that of growing up in an *invalidating environment.* To *invalidate* basically means to communicate that something is not valid, reasonable, understandable, or true. An invalidating environment is one in which people communicate that your thoughts and feelings are not valid, reasonable, understandable, or true. In an invalidating environment, you might also be punished, criticized, or ignored when you are upset (Linehan 1993a). Dr. Marsha Linehan's (1993a) theory is that the combination of emotionality and a childhood spent in an invalidating environment produces many of the problems of people with BPD.

Growing up in an invalidating environment can lead to many of the problems described by people with BPD. For instance, if your parents or caregivers got angry with you or punished you whenever you got really upset about something, you might have started to become afraid of your own emotions. Indeed, Dr. Linehan has said that many people with BPD are afraid of their own emotions (Linehan 1993a). Similarly, if you got upset because you felt hurt or criticized when your friend called you a derogatory name, and your parents got angry with you (for example, saying "Stop crying about it! There's no reason to be so upset. Go to your room!"), you might start to think that there was something wrong with your emotions. You might also think that there was something wrong with you for having these emotions in the first place, especially if someone is telling you that you shouldn't feel so upset. Indeed, people with BPD often have trouble trusting themselves and their emotions, and they often invalidate or chastise themselves for feeling so emotional.

Invalidating environments can also make a person feel out of control, because the environment provides feedback that may not be consistent with how the person thinks or feels about him-or herself. Some researchers have found that people prefer getting feedback from others that matches how they feel or think about themselves (Swann et al. 1990). Getting feedback that mirrors how you think or feel about yourself can be comforting; it might make you feel as if things make sense. In contrast, hearing something that does not fit your experience can be jarring and upsetting. Even people who have negative thoughts about themselves would rather hear negative things than positive things about themselves (Swann et al. 1990).

Similarly, when someone invalidates your feelings, your emotions might get stronger and feel out of control. If your brother just died and you were crying, and your friend said, "Come on, you weren't that close anyway. What's the matter with you?" you would probably feel irritated and sad, and you might get defensive. You might start trying to convince your friend that your feelings are valid, for example, by arguing with her or expressing your sadness more strongly. You might also bottle up your feelings whenever you are around your friend. People with BPD often go back and forth between bottling up and not expressing their feelings and exploding and expressing them very strongly. This could be one result of being invalidated repeatedly.

As we have mentioned, difficulty managing emotions is one of the most important features of BPD. And an invalidating environment does not teach a person how to manage his or her emotions (Linehan 1993a). In fact, being told that one's feelings are not correct or valid simply teaches a person to avoid emotions at all costs, and, as a result, emotions may start to seem scary. If you were in this environment, you might also punish yourself when you felt upset. Some people with BPD get caught in this vicious cycle. They express a strong feeling or do something that their partners don't like, feel ashamed for doing it, and then punish themselves, sometimes to avoid being punished by the people they are close to.

## *Problems with Attachment*

Another environmental factor has to do with problems with *attachment,* or the emotional bond that we have with other people. Many mental health professionals believe that healthy attachments to other people are essential for good mental health and fulfilling relationships. Some people even think that having a strong, secure attachment is the basis for developing all sorts of skills that help us cope with life and meet our needs.

Researchers have developed ingenious ways of figuring out what kind of attachments people have. Researchers sometimes examine attachment by bringing a mother and her child into a room and then have the mother leave the child with a stranger for a period. This is called the *strange situation* paradigm (Ainsworth, Bell, and Stayton 1971). Infants who have a healthy, strong attachment (called a *secure attachment)* to their mothers will actively explore the environment when they are alone or with the mother and may be friendly to the stranger when the mother is around, but they clearly prefer the mother to the stranger. They might also get upset when the mother leaves and seek physical comfort from her when she returns. The mothers of securely attached babies tend to be sensitive, and they respond consistently to their child's emotional needs.

Some people with BPD may not have had the types of relationships necessary for producing secure attachment styles (Silk, Wolf, and Ben-Ami 2005). For instance, one study found that people with BPD often describe their parents as indifferent, abusive, or overcontrolling (Parker et al. 1999). As Dr. Kenneth Silk and his colleagues have aptly pointed out, these types of descriptions are similar to the invalidating environment we described above (Silk, Wolf, and Ben-Ami 2005).

In fact, some people think that some difficulties in relationships with parents might produce a *disorganized attachment style.* Infants with disorganized attachment styles show conflicting responses to their mother and alternate between avoiding or resisting contact with the mother, and seeking closeness with her. They also seem to be dazed, confused, and apprehensive. This type of attachment style often occurs among maltreated children (Baer and Martinez 2006).

If you think about it, the disorganized attachment style sounds a lot like BPD. One of the symptoms of BPD is the tendency to go back and forth in your thinking about people you are close to. For example, at times you might think that your partner is the most wonderful person in the world, and at other times you might think,

"This is the most annoying, horrible person I could ever be with!" You might also feel somewhat confused in your relationships, and you might have conflicting feelings that you can't seem to reconcile. The bottom line here is that difficult experiences with caregivers might have contributed to some of your problems if you have BPD.

# Factors That Keep BPD Going

In addition to learning about factors that may have caused BPD in the first place, it is important for you to know what types of factors might help to maintain BPD over time. It is not entirely clear how or why BPD sticks around for those who have it. But we believe that a couple of factors might be involved in maintaining the problems related to BPD.

## *Chaotic or Adverse Life Events*

One such factor may be chaotic or adverse life events. In our experience, people with BPD encounter an overwhelmingly large number of unpleasant, stressful events and hassles. We have seen people who, over one week, have quit their jobs, had a death in the family, had a serious car accident, been abandoned by an intimate partner, fallen down the stairs, experienced public humiliation, and so on (Brown and Chapman 2007). In fact, Dr. Marsha Linehan (1993a) came up with the term *unrelenting crisis* to describe this tendency of people with BPD to experience an enormous number of extremely stressful events. You might have noticed this yourself. You might feel like the crises in your life never let up. They just keep coming, one after the other, with no break for you to recuperate or prepare yourself to deal with the next tragedy.

What types of stress happen most often for people with BPD? Conflict with other people is probably the most common stressor, and it is a common trigger of self-harm and suicidal behavior among people with BPD (Welch and Linehan 2002). In addition, some research has found that being rejected, failing at something, and being alone are common triggers for emotional distress among people with BPD (Stiglmayr et al. 2005).

Being constantly exposed to chaotic or stressful life events certainly may keep your problems going. If you are constantly under stress, you may find that you are easily irritated, emotionally vulnerable, and lacking in the resources needed to cope with life. As a result, you might resort to behaviors like self-harm, drug use, or suicide attempts in order to cope.

Indeed, when people are distressed, they are more likely to act on impulse and do things that may be harmful (Tice, Bratslavsky, and Baumeister 2001). When you are upset, you are likely to use your resources to get rid of your distress. This, however, leaves very few resources available to stop yourself from doing impulsive things (Muraven, Tice, and Baumeister 1998). Think about how you feel when you are lifting weights: people lifting heavy weights are more likely to drop them when someone adds a new weight, or when they are exhausted from completing many repetitions. Similarly, if you are constantly encountering stressful life events, you might find that your coping resources are so depleted that you turn to suicide attempts, self-harm, or drug use.

## *Reinforcement: Unfortunately, Problematic Behaviors Sometimes Work!*

Another factor that might keep BPD going is that many of the behaviors that go along with BPD work quite well in the short term. Remember that *behavioral dysregulation* is one of the features of BPD, and it includes impulsive behaviors, such as binge eating, risky sex, drug use, alcohol use, reckless driving, suicide attempts, self-harm, and so on. The problem is that many of these behaviors work very well to make people feel better, at least for a little while. We think that is why people continue to do them—if something works, you are likely to continue doing it.

This point brings us to the idea of *reinforcement.* Reinforcement is a term that psychologists use to describe any consequence that increases the likelihood that you will do something again in a similar situation. For example, if you have felt a strong sense of shame after your partner criticized you, and you cut yourself and felt better for a little while, you are probably more likely to cut yourself when your partner criticizes you in the future. Relief from your shame *reinforced* (strengthened) the cutting behavior.

Many behaviors that go along with BPD work in this way. For instance, drinking alcohol, taking various drugs, and binge eating can make you feel less distressed in the short term. When your behavior works to get rid of something unpleasant, *negative reinforcement* is at play. This means that you keep doing these behaviors because they help you get rid of something negative (such as emotional distress). Using drugs, harming yourself, or taking risks can also give you a sense of euphoria and relaxation, a happy mood, or feelings of excitement. In these cases, when your behavior works to produce something pleasant, *positive reinforcement* is at play. This means that you keep doing these behaviors because you're getting something positive out of them. It is quite likely that both positive reinforcement and negative reinforcement partly maintain BPD. The good news is that if you stop doing these behaviors, this type of reinforcement stops, and you can start to work on finding other ways to feel better or get excitement in life.

## *The Vicious Cycle of BPD*

As you can imagine, this kind of reinforcement can get you into a vicious circle. First you experience a really stressful event (for example, someone rejects you), and then you feel emotionally distressed (you feel ashamed, sad, and maybe a little angry). If you have BPD, you probably have a hard time figuring out how to make yourself feel better. So you resort to something like self-harm, drugs, or alcohol. You feel better after you drink, use drugs, or hurt yourself, but doing these things (1) doesn't help to solve your problem of being rejected and (2) leads to more problems and more stress in the future. And what are you going to do the next time you are stressed out? You'll likely engage in the very same problem behaviors that helped you feel better last time! See figure 3.1 for an illustration of this vicious circle.

*Figure 3.1* The Vicious Circle That Maintains BPD

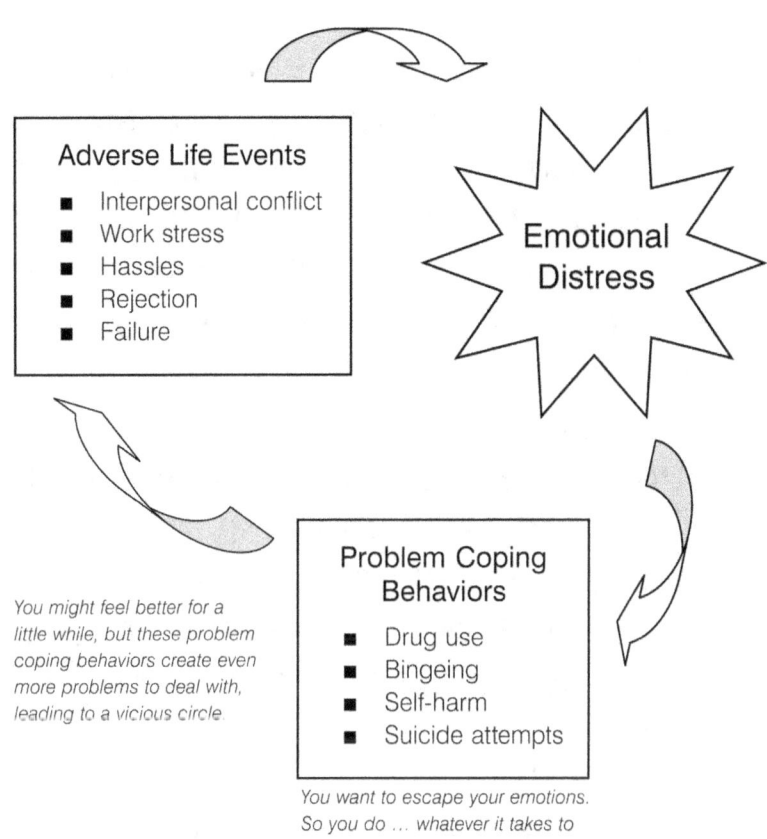

# Summary

In summary, many different factors work together in complex ways to cause and maintain BPD. Researchers have begun to unlock the puzzle of BPD, and we now know about some of the most important environmental and biological causes. Below is a summary of some of the main points to remember from this chapter.

- Biological causes related to BPD include heredity, genes, the size and functioning of brain areas (the amygdala, the hippocampus, and the prefrontal cortex), and neurotransmitters such as dopamine and serotonin.
- Personality traits related to BPD include emotional vulnerability, neuroticism, and impulsivity.
- Environmental causes related to BPD include childhood trauma, invalidating environments, and problems with attachment.
- Factors that maintain BPD may include adverse life events and reinforcement for dysregulated behaviors.

# 4
# Will I Have Borderline Personality Disorder Forever? The Course of BPD

*When Amy was in the hospital after she tried to kill herself, her psychiatrist told her she had BPD. At first, she was somewhat relieved to hear this—she felt like she finally had words to describe all of the pain she was going through and the problems she was having. She also felt less alone, knowing that there were other people with similar problems. After a couple of weeks at home, though, she started to get worried. What did this BPD thing actually mean? Was this something she was going to have to deal with forever? Was recovery possible? She quickly began to look for information that would tell her what to expect.*

When you are struggling with a psychiatric disorder, it is important to know just what to expect as the disorder progresses. Being diagnosed with a psychiatric disorder can be quite scary. First, as we have discussed, the general attitude toward people with mental illnesses is not always an enlightened one. On top of this, there is not a lot of accessible information on how long BPD lasts. And one of the scariest things for human beings is unpredictability. Not knowing how long you might have BPD or whether it is likely to go away can be really frightening. If you were to be diagnosed with cancer or heart disease, you would certainly want to know how long you should expect your illness to last, how intense it might get, which symptoms are likely to go away first, and which symptoms or problems might stick around for longer.

Simply having information about what to expect as a disorder progresses and how that disorder is likely to change (or not) over time can take away some of the uncertainty and unpredictability of the disorder, making it less scary and more manageable. What's more, knowing what to expect can help you plan ahead and prepare you to cope better in the future. For all these reasons, it is important to get as much information as possible about the likely progression of BPD over time, including the symptoms you can expect to change and those that are probably going to remain.

Not very long ago, people thought that BPD lasted forever. In fact, that is one of the reasons BPD is called a "personality disorder." The basic idea was that if BPD is part of someone's personality, it can be expected to continue throughout that person's life. And, in some ways, this made sense—if people's personalities are supposed to stay the same throughout their lives, then personality disorders should stay the same as well. However, we now know that personality disorders are not stable. In fact, it is probably safest to assume that disorders like BPD will change (or even go away) over time.

The idea that people may recover from personality disorders is relatively new and goes against many common myths. This is exactly why it is essential for you to read this chapter and get accurate information about the timeline (or *course*) of recovery from BPD.

Another important point to keep in mind is that the symptoms of BPD vary in their stability over time. Some symptoms seem to stick around for a long time, and others may get better or worse or may even go away at some point. Therefore, you can expect that some symptoms will change relatively quickly, and others may not change at all. Knowing which symptoms may change and which may not change will help you know what to expect in your recovery process.

# The Course of BPD: How Long It May Take to Recover

Although mental health professionals once thought that BPD was a lifelong disorder with little chance of recovery, this belief was based solely on ill-founded assumptions and anecdotal evidence (such as observations by some therapists that their patients with BPD didn't seem to get better) and had no basis in scientific research. In fact, up until recently, there was no scientific research to tell us how long BPD lasts. Over the last couple of decades, however, researchers have begun to study how this disorder plays out over time, following many people with this disorder to see how and when they recover. The results of two such long-term studies have provided us with cause for hope. In a nutshell, this research is showing us that once-held beliefs about the stability and incurability of BPD are completely wrong.

Specifically, there is now a lot of evidence that most people who are hospitalized with BPD will no longer meet criteria for this disorder (in other words, they will experience a *remission*) after six years. One study by Dr. Mary Zanarini and her colleagues (2003) found that 35 percent of people with BPD who were hospitalized for psychiatric difficulties no longer met criteria for BPD after as little as two years. What's more, almost half of the former inpatients (49 percent) did not meet criteria for BPD four years later, and 69 percent still did not meet criteria for BPD six years later. In fact, over the course of the six-year period, a full 74 percent of the patients who had started off with BPD no longer met criteria for BPD at some point during the study. Just as important, most people (94 percent) who had stopped meeting criteria for BPD never met criteria for BPD again during the rest of the study. In other words, BPD didn't go away just to flare back up again. For many people, it went away and stayed away. The other important point to keep in mind is that this study was not a treatment study, and it was not intended to examine the benefits of a particular treatment for BPD. Therefore, even though most patients continued to receive some form of psychological treatment over the course of the study, the kinds of treatment they received varied, and not everyone remained in treatment throughout the entire six years. In fact, some people were not in treatment at all. The reason this is important is that this tells us that even in the absence of a particular state-of-the-art treatment for BPD (like the treatments we will tell you more about in chapters 8 and 9), many people with BPD will eventually get better over time.

Another study has also looked at the timeline for BPD, in comparison with that for three other personality disorders and major depression (Gunderson et al. 2000; Skodol et al. 2005). At the time of publication, this study had passed the seven-year mark, and it had found a pattern similar to that found in the 2003 study by Dr. Zanarini and her colleagues. Specifically, over half the patients with BPD in their study stopped meeting criteria for BPD at some point within the first two years of the study. And, if that doesn't sound hopeful enough, consider this: over 25 percent of the patients with BPD reported almost no symptoms for more than a year, suggesting relatively complete recovery (Grilo et al. 2004). Also, this study found that 10 percent of patients with BPD stopped meeting criteria for BPD within the first six months of the study (Skodol et al. 2005). In contrast to the idea that BPD somehow sticks to you like glue, or like a tattoo that you can't remove, BPD may be far more changeable than we ever thought!

In fact, BPD may even be a diagnosis with more cause for hope than some others. For instance, disorders like depression and bipolar disorder often come back many times during a person's life. In contrast, recovery from BPD often means that it will not return in the same way.

So, that's the good news. Of course, the six-year recovery rate is not 100 percent; therefore, it is important to understand some of the things that make recovery from BPD slower, or interfere with recovery from BPD. For instance, it can be harder to recover from BPD if you have another psychiatric disorder as well, and (as we will discuss more in the next chapter) BPD is often accompanied by a variety of other psychiatric disorders. Consider this the "fine print" for BPD: "When purchasing BPD, please be aware that you'll get a lot more than you bargained for." Now let's turn our attention to some of the things that interfere with recovery from BPD.

# Factors That Interfere with Recovery from BPD

*Amy just didn't know where to begin. She kept asking herself, "How much more of this can I take?" As if having BPD wasn't hard enough, she struggled with depression and sometimes drank too much at night. When her drinking got too excessive or her depression was worse, she would wonder how she could possibly gather enough energy and motivation to do the things she needed to do in therapy. She often wished she didn't have to deal with so many problems all at once.*

Basically, what this section boils down to is this: the more problems you have, the harder it can be to address each of them. People generally find that having another psychological disorder on top of BPD makes recovery from

BPD slower and more challenging. In addition, certain disorders make it especially hard to recover from BPD.

## *Substance Use Disorders*

One type of disorder that most interferes with recovery from BPD is a substance use disorder. There are two types of substance use disorders: substance abuse and substance dependence. *Substance abuse* involves having difficulties in your life due to alcohol or drug use; and *substance dependence* involves being so preoccupied with alcohol or drug use that you think about it all the time, go to great lengths to get drugs or alcohol, or have a high tolerance for drugs or alcohol (in other words, you can take a lot of drugs or alcohol without getting too intoxicated), among other problems. In the study of the formerly hospitalized patients with BPD we discussed earlier, the researchers found that people who did not have a substance use disorder were four times more likely to stop meeting criteria for BPD at some point in the study (Zanarini, Frankenburg, et al., "Axis I comorbidity," 2004).

This tells us that a substance use disorder dramatically interferes with remission from BPD. Although we don't know exactly why this is the case, substance use problems generally compound people's problems and have many negative consequences. What's more, some of the negative consequences of substance abuse are very similar to some of the problems that people with BPD already struggle with. For example, substance abuse can lead to risky or reckless behavior, it can make people more emotional, and it can lead to problems with relationships. Sound familiar? Ironically, many people with BPD may actually use substances to escape from some of these problems and get temporary relief from emotional pain. Yet, in the long run, substance abuse is probably going to make these same problems even worse.

## Post-traumatic Stress Disorder

Another disorder that often goes along with BPD and seems to complicate recovery is PTSD (Zanarini, Frankenburg, et al., "Axis I comorbidity," 2004). As you may remember from chapter 3, PTSD is one of the disorders that can occur following the experience of a traumatic event. The reason these two disorders often go hand in hand is that many people with BPD have experienced traumatic events in their lives, including childhood abuse. So, the same events that may make someone more likely to have BPD also make someone more likely to have PTSD.

Exactly why having PTSD might make it harder to recover from BPD is not known, but there are a couple of possible explanations. First, if you have both PTSD and BPD, the stressful experiences you had growing up may be at the extreme and severe end of the spectrum. As we have discussed, many different kinds of stressful experiences can lead to BPD. These experiences range from not feeling like you fit in with your family and/or not getting the attention you need to severe physical and sexual abuse. However, because you can only have PTSD if you have experienced a traumatic event, chances are that people who have both BPD and PTSD had the most severe stressful experiences growing up. The fact that having both disorders may be a sign that you have survived particularly difficult and traumatic experiences may explain why it would be harder to recover from BPD.

Another reason PTSD may complicate recovery from BPD is that the problems that go along with having PTSD are similar to the problems that we see in BPD, and having "double doses" of the same types of problems can make it more difficult to deal with those problems. If someone were to break into your home and hit your brand-new coffee table with a steel hammer once, you might be very upset, but you could probably fix it and move on. If, however, this kept happening again and again, it would become a lot more difficult to fix the table. Similarly, because the problems that go along with PTSD are similar to those of BPD, each disorder can compound the problems of the other disorder.

For example, as we discussed before, many people consider emotion dysregulation to be one of the central problems of BPD. However, emotion dysregulation is also a part of PTSD. If you have both disorders, you might expect a double dose of emotion dysregulation, making it more difficult to recover from either disorder. The same could be expected to occur with the problem of avoidance. People with PTSD tend to avoid the situations and thoughts that remind them of the trauma they have experienced. And, as we have discussed, people with BPD tend to cope with their emotions by avoiding them. Because avoidance might keep you from facing your problems head-on, this double dose of avoidance might make it even harder for you to recover from BPD. As we discuss in greater detail below, recovering from BPD seems to require active problem solving, and avoidance of any sort seems to interfere with progress.

## *Mood and Anxiety Disorders*

The presence of mood and anxiety disorders, major depression and panic disorder in particular, also interferes with recovery from BPD (Zanarini, Frankenburg, et al., "Axis I comorbidity," 2004). If you have either of these emotional disorders, it could mean that you are more emotionally vulnerable or have even more difficulty managing your emotions than if you had BPD alone. This could explain why it would take a little longer for you to recover from BPD. Also, just like with PTSD, people with panic disorder and depression do many things to avoid their emotions. For example, people with panic disorder tend to avoid going places where they fear they might have a panic attack. Although all of us avoid anxiety or other emotions at times, avoiding or trying not to feel these emotions can actually make them worse. If you have this problem, you may have noticed that the more you try to avoid anxiety or anxiety-provoking events, the scarier life becomes.

In another example of how mood and anxiety disorders might lead to avoidance, people who are depressed tend to withdraw and isolate themselves from others, basically avoiding activities. However, in order to deal with depression you have to do the exact opposite of this—you need to get more active (Jacobson et al. 1996). So, depression and anxiety disorders (such as panic disorder) might make it harder to recover from BPD because the avoidance that goes along with these disorders kindles the fires of emotional pain and prevents you from doing the very things that would help you recover.

## *Other Personality Disorders*

Finally, the presence of another set of personality disorders also seems to interfere with remission from BPD. Specifically, when people with BPD also meet criteria for an *anxious-fearful* personality disorder, they are more likely to continue to meet criteria for BPD after six years (Zanarini,

Frankenburg, et al., "Axis II comorbidity," 2004). According to the *DSM-IV-TR,* there are three different personality disorders considered to be anxious-fearful personality disorders:
- *Avoidant personality disorder,* characterized by extreme shyness in social situations, feelings of inadequacy, fears of disapproval and rejection by others, and great sensitivity to negative evaluation by others
- *Dependent personality disorder,* characterized by a strong need to be taken care of and fears of abandonment or separation from others (which leads to "clinging behavior" or submissiveness in relationships)
- *Obsessive-compulsive personality disorder,* characterized by a preoccupation with orderliness, perfectionism, and control that is so extreme and pervasive that it interferes with openness, flexibility, and getting things done efficiently

Some people have suggested that underlying each of these personality disorders is an *inhibited temperament.*

People with inhibited temperaments tend to be cautious and anxious in new situations, and they are often shy and not especially outgoing. So, how would having a more inhibited temperament interfere with recovery from BPD? Well, recovery from BPD takes a lot of very hard work. It requires a lot of energy and involves a lot of personal risk. It is easier to recover from BPD if you are willing to seek support and put yourself out there. For people who were born more shy and anxious, it can be difficult to work up the nerve and energy to throw themselves into the recovery process. For this reason, people who were born a bit more active and outgoing may have a leg up in recovering from BPD.

So, what does this mean if you are one of those people who just happens to be more shy? It does not mean that you won't be able to recover from BPD. What it does mean, though, is that recovery may be more difficult for you, and you may need to push yourself more than other people have to. In fact, if you know that you are naturally shy, use what you have learned here as your motivation to be more active and to seek the support you need.

## Changes Across Different Types of BPD Symptoms

As we mentioned before, the symptoms of BPD fall into five main categories: emotional, interpersonal, cognitive, identity/self, and behavioral. Most people with BPD struggle with all of these areas, having problems with their emotions, thoughts, and relationships, and often engaging in risky behaviors. Some of these symptoms may be considered part of your personality. For instance, you may have always been an emotional person, and you may always be an emotional person. There's absolutely nothing wrong with that. The problem seems to arise when you do certain things to deal with your emotions, such as using drugs or harming yourself.

You could think of emotionality as a personality trait—a key ingredient in the mix that makes you who you are. If you have an emotional personality or temperament, we might not expect that to change very much. In contrast, the things you do when you are upset or in a crisis—attempting suicide, using drugs, or hurting yourself—may be more likely to change. These behaviors are not who you are; they are things you may do in the moment to cope with problems you have.

So, what does this have to do with BPD? Well, it turns out that certain symptoms of BPD change more quickly than others, and this might have to do with whether the symptoms are part of your personality, or simply the way you go about coping with your distress.

What symptoms can you expect to improve the most? As we mentioned above, the research seems to show that the behavioral symptoms of BPD (such as risky behaviors) change more than others. In the study by Dr. Zanarini and her colleagues (2003) that we discussed earlier, only one-quarter of the patients with BPD reported self-harm or suicidal behavior after six years, even though 80 percent had these behaviors at the start of the study. This is a dramatic decrease and a very good sign, given how risky these behaviors are. Similarly, by the six-year mark, the percentage of patients abusing substances was only 25 percent, down from 50 percent. What this tells us is that if you have BPD, you can expect your behavioral symptoms to change most quickly and to be reduced the most through treatment (compared to the other symptoms of BPD).

On the other hand, if you are diagnosed with BPD, you probably should not expect your emotional symptoms to change too much. The majority of patients with BPD were still experiencing the emotional symptoms of BPD six years later, although most of these people no longer met criteria for BPD (Zanarini et al. 2003). As we explained previously, these emotional symptoms include intense feelings of depression, hopelessness, guilt, anger, anxiety, loneliness, and emptiness. The fact that the patients continued to have these emotions may reflect the fact that people with BPD are simply hardwired to be more emotionally intense and to experience their emotions more strongly. Although these emotions can be painful, they don't have to interfere with your life, and, in the absence of other difficulties, they are not signs of psychological problems; instead, they may simply reflect someone's temperament.

So, what does this tell us? First, it tells us that you should probably not expect some of your emotional symptoms to change as much, and should not consider yourself or your treatment a failure if they don't. These emotions may simply remain with you throughout your life, and they don't have to keep you from having the life you want. Of course, this does not mean that you are always going to feel as terrible as you do now, or that you will always be in as much emotional turmoil. In fact, we believe that the more you learn to control your impulsive behaviors, manage your relationships, and develop the life you want, the better you are going to feel overall.

The point we are trying to make here is twofold. First, everyone experiences negative emotions. It is not possible to be human and alive and not sometimes feel sad, anxious, angry, lonely, and so on. To be human means to feel emotions, and many of these emotions are negative. We just really want to stress the fact that even with the best and most successful treatment, people will always have negative emotions, because this is part of being alive.

The other point we want to make is that some people are simply born more emotionally intense than others. They feel things more strongly and experience their emotions more intensely. This is just the way they are, a part of their personality. And, because it is a part of their personality, this is probably not going to change. So, if you are someone who is more emotionally intense than other people are, you are probably always going to feel things more strongly. And that is not a bad thing and does not have to hurt your life in any way.

The other thing that this research tells us is that you might get "more bang for your buck," so to speak, by focusing in treatment on changing how you cope with your feelings and the problems in your life, rather than spending all of your energy trying not to feel certain things, or trying to get rid of your emotions. It's just not possible to get rid of your emotions, and trying to do that is really a fruitless battle. Besides, we think that getting your behaviors under control and learning new ways of coping with your problems will actually make you feel better and help you have the life you want. So, by focusing your energy on changing how you cope with your emotions and the problems in your life, you are probably going to see better results than you would if you tried to change a part of your personality or temperament.

The rate of change for problems with thoughts and relationships falls somewhere between that for behavioral and emotional symptoms (Zanarini et al. 2003). Some of these symptoms seem to change pretty quickly, and others seem to be more like the emotional symptoms of BPD—long lasting and part of one's personality. Among the cognitive symptoms, severe forms of paranoid thinking changed the most over the course of six years, but other types of thoughts (negative beliefs about oneself and the world, such as "I am a terrible person" and "No one will ever like me") and dissociative symptoms remained fairly common.

As for interpersonal symptoms, the ones that changed the most quickly were the ones that are similar to the behavioral symptoms we talked about before, taking the form of impulsive behaviors within relationships. These symptoms included things like severe difficulties with therapists, unstable and stormy relationships, and the tendency to place extreme demands on other people. These symptoms probably cause quite a few problems in people's lives, and so it is really good news that they seem to improve pretty quickly. On the other hand, other interpersonal symptoms have an emotional component, like fears of abandonment and difficulties tolerating being alone, and so they tend to stick around longer.

Below is a snapshot of the symptoms that are most likely to improve over time:
- Impulsive, risky behaviors, including self-harm and suicide attempts

- Severe paranoid thinking
- Unstable, stormy relationships and the tendency to place extreme demands on other people

And here is a snapshot of the symptoms that are least likely to improve over time:

- Some emotional symptoms, such as depression, anxiety, anger, sadness, guilt, and emptiness
- Dissociative episodes and negative beliefs about oneself or the world
- Fears of abandonment and difficulties tolerating being alone

In summary, the different symptoms of BPD don't change at the same time, or at the same pace. Some symptoms change pretty quickly and seem to improve pretty easily with treatment. Other symptoms can be thought of as personality traits, and these might stick around for a lot longer—possibly even throughout your life. The good news, though, is that the symptoms that are the most severe and that seem to wreak the most havoc in people's lives (like self-harm and suicidal behaviors, stormy relationships, and extreme paranoid beliefs) are the very same symptoms that appear to change the most quickly and may be reduced the most by treatment.

## Relationships Between the Different Symptoms of BPD

One last thing we want to mention is that even though we've been talking about the different types of symptoms in BPD and how they change at different paces (some fairly quickly, and others not much at all), all of these symptoms are related to one another. In fact, all of the symptoms of BPD influence one another. Think about it: it's probably not too surprising that if people learn to cope in ways other than hurting themselves, their relationships will get better. In fact, a lot of the impulsive behaviors that people with BPD struggle with can be difficult for other people to witness, and, therefore, can cause problems in relationships. It just makes sense: if you care about someone, it can be very difficult to watch that person do things that may hurt or even kill her or him. And, if that person kept doing those things over and over, you might start to get upset about that, possibly even yelling at that person or avoiding spending time with her or him. On the other hand, if you learn to control your impulsive behaviors and cope in other ways, your relationships are probably going to be much more stable. So, improvements in one area are probably going to cause improvements in other areas.

This is particularly likely to be true for the interpersonal symptoms of BPD. Some researchers think that the quality of a person's interpersonal relationships has a big influence on the symptoms and course of BPD (Gunderson 1984). The idea is that if people with BPD have stable, supportive relationships, they are likely to get better quicker. In fact, studies have found that some people with BPD show dramatic improvements in a short time after they end very stressful relationships or develop more supportive relationships (Gunderson et al. 2003).

It may not be surprising that people tend to do better when they have a good support system and people to rely on. However, we really want to emphasize this point because some people with BPD are tempted to withdraw from relationships over time. If your relationships are troubled and unstable, you may find yourself considering giving up on relationships altogether. Although this decision would probably lead to less interpersonal chaos (and potentially less relationship-related emotional pain), that does not mean it is the healthiest thing to do. Because human beings are social creatures and need support and social contact to thrive, it may be most helpful for recovery to work to develop some healthy relationships, rather than to avoid relationships altogether.

## Summary

BPD is a diagnosis with much more cause for hope than we once thought. Many people with BPD recover in only a few years, and, once they recover, their symptoms are unlikely to return. Of course, not everyone recovers at the same rate, and it is important to understand the types of things that make recovery more difficult. One of these things is having another psychiatric disorder in addition to BPD. The more problems you have, the harder it can be to address them all, and having another disorder on top of BPD makes recovery from BPD slower. In particular, having a substance use disorder, PTSD, panic disorder, depression, or one of the anxious-fearful personality disorders makes it especially hard to recover from BPD.

Another thing to remember is that not all of the symptoms of BPD change at exactly the same pace. If you have BPD, you can expect that some of your symptoms will change fairly quickly, and others might stick around for a lot longer—possibly throughout your entire life. The reason for this is that some symptoms of BPD (such as how intensely you feel your emotions and how sensitive you are to the things around you) can be thought of as simply a part of your personality. Because these symptoms are part of your personality, we wouldn't expect them to change very much. In contrast, other symptoms of BPD involve things you may do when you are struggling or having a crisis of some sort (such as attempting suicide, impulsively using drugs, and hurting yourself). These behaviors are things you may do, not who you are; for this reason, they are much more likely to change. And, this is really good news, because it means that the symptoms of BPD that hurt you and your loved ones the most (like self-harm and suicidal behaviors, and stormy relationships) are the very same symptoms that treatments can alleviate the most.

# 5

# Problems That Often Go Along with Borderline Personality Disorder

*Tom's life felt out of control. For as long as he could remember, he had struggled with his emotions. Even the smallest thing would set him off, sending him into a panic, rage, or severe depression. The only time he felt okay was when he was high. At first, smoking pot seemed like the perfect solution. He would chill out, relax, and feel less anxious around people. But recently he had started to feel out of control. Even when he didn't plan on using, he somehow couldn't resist. He would tell himself he was going to take a night off, only to find himself getting high before he even realized what was happening! And now, with last night's fiasco, he didn't know what he was going to do. How could he have been so careless? Why didn't he think before getting into his car and driving after a night of smoking pot? It was then that he realized that what had seemed like a solution was only a bigger problem, and now he was really out of control.*

As we have discussed throughout this book, the symptoms of BPD are very distressing. People who suffer from this disorder often feel like they are out of control. They may feel as if their emotions are their enemies, serving no other purpose than to make their lives miserable. Having such overwhelming emotions, thoughts, behaviors, and interpersonal relationships is enough to make life a struggle. Unfortunately, many people with BPD have not only this disorder to contend with but other psychiatric disorders and problems as well. In this chapter, we discuss the different types of disorders and problems that tend to go along with BPD, as well as possible reasons why this may be the case.

# Psychiatric Disorders That Often Co-Occur with BPD

As we mentioned in chapter 4, BPD comes with a lot of baggage. Most people with BPD have at least one other psychiatric disorder, and some of them have several other disorders. If you have BPD, you may have noticed that, in addition to this disorder, you also have problems with depression or anxiety, or struggle with alcohol or drug use. As we mentioned before, having to cope with the symptoms of multiple psychiatric disorders can be quite a challenge, and it can make recovering from BPD even more difficult. Therefore, it is very important to understand the disorders that often go along with BPD.

## *Substance Use*

Substance abuse and dependence are very common among people with BPD. Studies have found that as many as two-thirds of people with BPD also have substance use problems (Lieb, Zanarini, et al. 2004), and approximately one-fifth of people who abuse substances meet criteria for BPD (Trull et al. 2000). So, why do BPD and substance abuse seem to go hand in hand?

**Escaping and Avoiding Emotional Pain**

The answer to this question may lie in the very understandable desire to avoid emotional pain. Quite simply, substances provide an escape from emotional pain. As we discussed before, wanting to avoid or escape distressing emotions is perfectly normal. Most of us don't start the day saying, "I hope this day is full of anxiety!" or "I can't wait for a week full of heartache!" When we are upset, we often want to get away from those feelings as quickly as possible.

One way to get away from these feelings is to avoid whatever it is that is causing us distress. For example, when people are sad, they may call a friend to take their mind off their sadness. When people are anxious, they may count to ten or take deep breaths to get away from their anxiety. When people are angry, they may leave the situation that is making them angry. All of these examples have one thing in common: when we experience distressing or uncomfortable feelings, we often want to get away from these feelings and the situations that bring them up.

**Problems with Avoiding and Escaping Emotional Pain**

Even though the desire to avoid emotional distress is normal, there are some problems that go along with avoiding or escaping uncomfortable feelings. One of these is that avoiding your feelings doesn't help you deal with the problems that led to these feelings in the first place.

Have you ever found yourself feeling really upset about something and then doing everything in your power to avoid feeling this way? Let's say that you got a poor performance review at work and your boss told you that you have to start arriving at work earlier and doing your work more efficiently. When you heard this, you felt distressed—maybe sad, anxious, or even a little ashamed of your performance. If you then completely avoided these feelings by using drugs or drinking every morning before work, you might feel a little better in the moment, but good luck keeping your job! If, however, you paid attention to how you were feeling, and you gave some thought to how to do better at work, you might get a better review next time. And, if you did get a better review, you wouldn't feel so upset the next time around. As you can see, one problem with avoiding emotions (especially through drugs) is that it stops you from facing and solving your problems. Your problems stick around, making you more upset, and you get caught in a vicious circle of avoiding and escaping while your problems continue to pile up.

Another problem with avoiding emotions is related to the fact that people with BPD tend to be more emotional than many other people are. As we've said before, there's nothing wrong with being an emotional person. In fact, if you are very emotional, you may live a richer and fuller life than people who aren't as emotional. On the other hand, some of the typical coping strategies that other people use to deal with emotions or thoughts may not work for you. That is, because you have such strong emotions, you probably need something really strong to help you cope with your emotions. As a result, you may sometimes find yourself at a loss for how to deal with your distressing feelings. In fact, we think that's why some people with BPD resort to substance abuse.

Think about it: substances such as alcohol, marijuana, prescription drugs, or heroin cause people to enter an *altered state*— a mental state in which you don't feel like yourself. You may feel more confident, happy, calm, or simply numb. More often than not, people with BPD use substances to gain temporary relief from intense feelings and thoughts that are difficult to tolerate. But the key word here is *temporary.*

## Problems with Using Drugs or Alcohol to Avoid or Escape Emotional Pain

A major problem with using substances to escape is that this escape is very short lived, and afterward you may feel even worse than you did beforehand. Basically, the very thing you used to make yourself feel better ends up making you feel even worse later on. And what do you think you're going to want to do when you feel worse? Use more drugs or alcohol, of course! That's the problem.

Another problem is that the more you use drugs and alcohol, the more likely you are to build up a *tolerance* for these substances, so that eventually you need a larger amount of your chosen substance to get the same effect. When you were eighteen and experimenting with alcohol, two beers might have been enough to get you drunk. But, after drinking for a few years, you might require a six-pack to get the same effect.

And, if you use a substance long enough, you may experience *withdrawal symptoms,* the body's reaction to not having the substance, often followed by a craving for the substance and uncomfortable physical feelings (such as agitation, anxiousness, sweating, and nausea, among others). Once this starts happening, people may actually start to use drugs and alcohol simply to get rid of the withdrawal symptoms themselves. At this point, the substance essentially begins to control the person's life. Relationships may suffer, responsibilities at work may not be met, and health problems may develop.

With all of these negative consequences, why would anyone continue to use substances, much less abuse them? Well, the temporary relief that substances provide can be so great that people who are in extreme emotional pain may be willing to risk these longer-term negative consequences. Having intense emotional pain and few ways to manage that pain can make you desperate for anything that will provide even temporary relief—even if this means that you have to deal with worse consequences later on. Immediate relief, even if it's short lived, is a powerful incentive if you are in tremendous pain.

**The Good News**

The good news is that because BPD and substance use so often go hand in hand, many popular treatments for BPD make a point of dealing with substance use. For example, dialectical behavior therapy (DBT; Linehan 1993a) has been used to treat people with both BPD and substance use disorders and has been found to work well (Linehan et al. 1999). In short, DBT assumes that substance use is something people with BPD do to cope with distress. Thus, DBT involves teaching people with BPD other ways to cope with and tolerate unpleasant feelings. The basic idea is that if you learn more effective ways to deal with emotional pain, you may be less likely to turn to drastic and unhealthy ways of coping with feelings, such as substance use.

## *Eating Disorders*

Eating disorders are also quite common among individuals with BPD. Studies have found that as many as 50 percent of people with BPD have an eating disorder (Lieb, Zanarini, et al. 2004). Eating disorders generally take the form of either *anorexia nervosa* (restricting food intake to such a degree that the person is severely underweight) or *bulimia nervosa* (a cycle of bingeing and purging where large amounts of food are consumed and then eliminated through vomiting, overexercising, and/or laxative abuse). As is the case with substance use problems, there are some very good reasons why so many people with BPD struggle with an eating disorder.

**Escaping and Avoiding Emotional Pain**

The first reason is similar to the one we discussed above regarding substance use problems, and it is most relevant to bulimia. Like substance use, both bingeing and purging can be ways of coping with emotional distress and relieving negative emotions. Think about it—eating is one of the most common ways people soothe themselves. Even people who do not have an eating disorder often use food to provide comfort during times of stress or distress. How many times have you or has someone you know turned to food for comfort when feeling down, or sad, or lonely, or upset? Indeed, clinical researchers have suggested that the tendency for people to use food for comfort may help explain the high rates of obesity in the United States (Dallman et al. 2003).

In fact, just like with substances, the desire to use food to provide emotional relief may even have a biological basis. Certain types of foods, such as breads, cakes, chips, cookies, and candy (the very types of foods that people are most likely to binge on), can actually improve your mood, leading to temporary relaxation, comfort, and an overall sense of calmness. Eating these sugary or fatty foods actually works on the "pleasure center" of your brain, causing the release of dopamine, similar to the effects of some drugs. So, it is not surprising that, like many others, people with BPD often turn to food to soothe themselves and relieve their distress.

Just like with substances, though, there are serious problems with relying on binge eating to cope with distress. Although bingeing can provide temporary relief from emotional pain, it can become an addiction over time. Basically, the more people eat to cope with their feelings, the more they need to eat in order to get the same emotional relief—leading to more and more binges, as well as an increasing sense of being out of control. And if you have bulimia in particular, the more you binge, the more you are going to feel the need to purge (by vomiting, taking laxatives, or exercising excessively). Purging is very dangerous and can lead to major health problems. What's more, it doesn't work! Some research has shown that vomiting after a meal gets rid of only about one-third of the calories that were consumed (Kaye et al. 1993).

So, this cycle of bingeing to deal with emotions, and purging to avoid weight gain, is a vicious one that can take over your life. In fact, after a while, some people find that they start to spend almost all of their time going back and forth between bingeing and purging. What's more, to add to the addictive nature of bulimia, purging can provide temporary relief from emotional pain, as people sometimes experience a release of tension or calmness following an episode of purging. This relief can be so strong that it makes people more prone to bingeing and purging in the future, despite the likely harm to their relationships, their health, and their lives.

**Body Dissatisfaction**

A second reason that eating disorders are common among people with BPD may have to do with body dissatisfaction. Although eating disorders are not solely the result of a poor body image or desire to be thin, most people with eating disorders are displeased with their bodies and dislike the way they look. Because many people with BPD have had negative childhood experiences, it is not uncommon for them to have experienced emotional abuse. And, one form of emotional abuse may include negative remarks about a person's looks or self. If you grew up in a family where you were taught that you were not good enough, you might have grown up hating everything about yourself. One thing about ourselves that can be especially easy to dislike in our body-and image-conscious society is our bodies. All around us, we get the message that it is best to be thin. If you grew up hating yourself and your body, you may be even more likely to buy into the message that thinness is the ideal.

The behaviors that go along with eating disorders—purging and restricting food intake—can be a person's dramatic attempts to alter her or his body shape and weight, as a result of body dissatisfaction. What's more, because behaviors like bingeing and purging can take such a toll on the body (leading to health problems and bodily harm), they can be a way of expressing and acting out self-hatred. Thus, body dissatisfaction is another reason eating disorders may be common among people with BPD.

**Sense of Control**

One of the things that can be most distressing for human beings in general is a lack of control. If you have BPD, you may feel like your life, emotions, relationships, and behaviors are out of control. As a result, you might feel desperate to find some way of controlling at least a small part of your life. An eating disorder like anorexia nervosa may be common among people with BPD because this disorder can provide people with a much-needed sense of control (given that we all have final say over when we eat and how much we eat). Although this sense of control is actually an illusion, since eating disorders usually take on a life of their own and become out of control, purposefully restricting food intake and choosing not to eat can provide people with a momentary sense of control over at least some aspect of their lives.

In fact, it's probably not a coincidence that refusing to eat is something that most people would find very hard to do. Humans need food to live, and it is a basic human instinct to eat until full. When people don't eat enough, they can feel weak, tired, and dizzy, and they can have difficulty functioning. Therefore, it is very difficult to continuously refrain from eating. This is one of the things that makes diets so difficult! Anyhow, because it is such a hard thing to do and because most people do not do so easily, restricting food intake can make someone feel like they are really powerful and in control. This can be quite a reassuring experience when your life feels out of control! Again, the problem is that this control is not real and that intensive food restriction can soon become very out of control. However, the desire to have control and to exert this over one's life is completely understandable and a basic human need.

## *Depression*

Many people with BPD also experience depression. Depression is more than just sadness. Depression refers to a set of symptoms that together cause tremendous impairment, including the following:
- Intense sadness and hopelessness
- Loss of pleasure in formerly enjoyable activities
- Suicidal thoughts
- Low self-esteem
- Appetite and sleep changes (too much or too little)
- Concentration difficulties
- Low motivation and energy

Depression is probably one of the most common disorders found among people with BPD. In fact, studies have found that 41 to 87 percent of people with BPD also struggle with depression (Lieb, Zanarini, et al. 2004; Zanarini, Frankenburg, et al., "Axis I comorbidity," 2004).

In order to understand why depression is so common among people with BPD, let's review the symptoms of BPD. People with BPD often have difficult relationships, which may be characterized by arguments, breakups, and even abuse. In addition, many people with BPD have intense fears that they will be abandoned. People with BPD experience negative emotions frequently and intensely and may feel as though there is nothing they can do to cope with these emotions. They may not have much of a sense of who they are, and they may worry that others are talking about them behind their backs or are not supportive of them. Finally, treatment for BPD may be a difficult and painful process.

When you look at all of these symptoms together, you can probably see why someone with BPD could start to feel depressed. Indeed, if you have BPD, the symptoms you experience may be so intense and long-standing that you might feel that there is nothing that can help you. You might also begin to believe that there is no point in continuing to waste time or energy on trying to get better. In addition, as a result of stormy relationships and constant fighting with the people around you, you might start to feel really isolated and lonely. Basically, the problems that go along with BPD are often the exact ingredients that can lead to depression.

If depression is indeed a side effect of having BPD, you might expect your depression to lessen once you recover from BPD, and you would be right. In fact, Dr. Gunderson and his colleagues (2004) found that decreases in BPD symptoms over time are followed by reductions in depression (rather than vice versa). This study supports the idea that depression stems from the painful symptoms of BPD. It also shows that if your BPD symptoms get better, your depression might get better also.

## Bipolar Disorder

Approximately 10 percent of people with BPD have bipolar disorder (Zanarini, Frankenburg, et al., "Axis I comorbidity," 2004). Bipolar disorder is actually a category of several disorders that share a common feature. Generally, people with bipolar disorder experience extreme fluctuations in their moods. If you have bipolar disorder, you might experience a period of depression that lasts for a couple of weeks or longer, and then swing up into a state called *mania,* during which you might feel like you're on top of the world, very powerful, and/or able to accomplish huge undertakings (such as writing a novel). You might also have a ton of energy, or be especially irritable. When people are in the manic phase of a bipolar disorder, they tend to be very impulsive and they usually get very little sleep. There are several different types of bipolar disorder, but all involve extreme mood swings. Thus, because this kind of emotional dysfunction is so common in BPD, it is not surprising that some people with BPD also have a type of bipolar disorder.

## The Problem of Misdiagnosis

*Treatment just didn't seem to be working for Katie. When she was hospitalized after trying to kill herself, Katie was diagnosed with bipolar disorder. At first, she found comfort in the fact that everything she struggled with was common enough to have its own name. And, once she heard that mood stabilizers usually helped people with bipolar disorder, she was hopeful that she would finally start to feel better. The problem was, treatment just didn't seem to be clicking. She still felt like she was on an emotional roller-coaster ride, and she often found herself thinking about suicide. And, no matter how much she tried, she just couldn't relate to the other members of her bipolar disorders therapy group. Their experiences just didn't resonate with hers. It wasn't until she started working with her new therapist that she learned that she'd been given the wrong diagnosis and was receiving the wrong treatment.*

One problem with the apparent similarities between BPD and bipolar disorder is that the two disorders are often confused. We have seen many people come to treatment with a diagnosis of bipolar disorder only to find out that they actually have BPD. One reason for this confusion is that mood swings are a symptom of both BPD and bipolar disorder. And the fact that there are different types of bipolar disorder makes matters even more confusing. Although some types of bipolar disorder involve major swings in mood that last a long time (for example, being depressed or manic for two weeks or longer), other types involve much more rapid shifts in mood—mood shifts that can look a lot like the up-and-down moods you might experience if you have BPD. So, someone might think that you have BPD when you really have bipolar disorder, or vice versa.

Despite the confusion, there is a definite difference between the mood swings in bipolar disorder and those in BPD. The mood swings in bipolar disorder generally do not occur as quickly as they often do among people with BPD. For example, someone with bipolar disorder may feel elated for a couple of days and then experience a sharp drop in mood to depression, but someone with BPD may shift from mood to mood in a matter of minutes or hours. However, among clinicians who are not familiar with BPD, the mood swings and impulsive behaviors of BPD could be mistaken for the mood swings and manic symptoms of bipolar disorder, resulting in the wrong diagnosis.

Of course, another reason people with BPD may sometimes be diagnosed with bipolar disorder instead of BPD is less about confusion and more about stigma. Basically, because of some of the myths about BPD we discussed in chapter 2, some clinicians would rather diagnose someone with bipolar disorder, in the hope that this disorder carries less stigma. Now, don't get us wrong—we appreciate the desire not to stigmatize people. But would you want to be given the wrong diagnosis? Probably not. Getting the wrong diagnosis can stop you from understanding what you are struggling with, and, even more important, it could lead you down the wrong treatment path. Therefore, we strongly believe that it is best to provide people with accurate diagnoses.

## *Anxiety Disorders*

In addition to mood disorders like depression, BPD is often accompanied by anxiety disorders (Lenzenweger et al., forthcoming; Zanarini, Frankenburg, et al., "Axis I comorbidity," 2004). There are quite a few anxiety disorders, including panic disorder, social anxiety disorder, obsessive-compulsive disorder, specific phobia, and post-traumatic stress disorder (PTSD). The most common anxiety disorders found among people with BPD are social anxiety disorder, panic disorder, and PTSD (Lieb, Zanarini, et al. 2004). For example, studies have found that one-quarter to one-half of people with BPD also experience social anxiety disorder, one-third to one-half also experience panic disorder, and approximately one-half also experience

PTSD (Lieb, Zanarini, et al. 2004). Below, we'll discuss possible reasons why each of these three anxiety disorders might be so common among people with BPD.

## Social Anxiety Disorder

First, let's take a look at *social anxiety disorder,* which involves intense fears of being negatively evaluated in social situations. For example, people with this disorder may fear giving a talk in front of people for fear of humiliating themselves. They may also fear other social situations, such as meeting new people, eating in front of people, or going to parties. As a result of these fears, people with social anxiety disorder often avoid these situations.

So, why does social anxiety disorder often go along with BPD? One possibility has to do with the relationship problems common among people with BPD. Basically, as a result of stressful, difficult, even abusive experiences with others, people with BPD may become anxious around others and hesitant to communicate their thoughts and feelings. As a result, they may not have a lot of confidence in interpersonal situations. In addition, as we discussed in chapter 3, some theories of the causes of BPD emphasize the significance of invalidation during childhood (Linehan 1993a). If you had invalidating experiences repeatedly, you might become afraid of expressing yourself around other people. You might even become less trusting of others, and you could develop anxiety about being in social situations, especially situations where you might be scrutinized by other people.

## Panic Disorder

Now let's turn our attention to *panic disorder,* a condition defined by the experience of recurrent and unexpected panic attacks, or sudden bursts of intense anxiety accompanied by particular kinds of fears, such as a fear of dying or losing control. Before we go into the ways in which BPD may be associated with panic disorder, it is important that we first provide a little more detail about how panic disorder develops.

Our bodies are hardwired to respond quickly to stressful situations. Called the "fight-or-flight" response, this is basically a survival mechanism. When we are faced with some kind of threat (real or imagined), our body prepares us to either fight or flee the situation. You will know this response is turned on when you begin to experience a rapid heartbeat, sweating, "tunnel vision" (where your attention becomes focused on only one thing—like getting out of a scary situation), muscle tension, and rapid breathing. Your body is essentially getting prepared for some kind of action. Again, this is a normal response.

However, sometimes this response can misfire. When we are very stressed out or haven't been taking care of ourselves, our fight-or-flight system might fire without any threat being present. This would be called a panic attack. Because there is no threat present, the panic attack seems like it comes "out of the blue" and, therefore, it can be very frightening. People who have panic attacks may think that they are having a heart attack, going crazy, or about to pass out. However, a panic attack does not mean any of these things. Instead, it probably means that you are stressed out, have not been taking care of yourself so well, and are scared of being anxious. When these things combine, the slightest twinge of anything even resembling anxiety can set off a chain reaction of more and more fear and arousal, until eventually you have a panic attack.

Panic attacks that occur without any warning are frightening because they are unpredictable. Human beings simply don't respond well to things that are unpredictable and uncontrollable. And this includes emotions like panic and fear: we'd generally rather know when to expect certain feelings and the kinds of things that might cause us to feel that way than to have these feelings hit us suddenly like a ton of bricks. In fact, because panic attacks are so scary, people may start to avoid situations that they think might lead to a panic attack. What's more, many people avoid going to places that they think might be difficult to escape from if they started to have a panic attack (such as a mall far from home). Other people avoid leaving their homes due to fears about having a panic attack in an unfamiliar place. This kind of avoidance can get so extreme that people may refuse to leave their house at all. This is called *agoraphobia*.

So how does this all apply to BPD? Simply because of the nature of BPD and its symptoms, people who have this disorder may experience heightened levels of stress. If you have BPD, your relationships are probably more stressful than other people's relationships. In fact, as we mentioned in chapter 3, your life in general may be more stressful. What's more, because people with BPD often have difficulties managing their emotions, your emotions may feel out of control, overly intense, and unpredictable. This is likely going to increase your stress levels and interfere with your ability to cope with stress on a daily basis. As a result, your body's fight-or-flight response may misfire, and you might have a panic attack. In fact, research suggests that emotional difficulties, and the stress associated with having these difficulties, do increase the likelihood that someone will have a panic attack (Manfo et al. 1996). And, unfortunately, if a panic attack occurs once, it is quite likely that this will lead to worries and fears about future panic attacks, as well as avoidance of any situation or experience that could lead to another panic attack. Because people with BPD already have a tendency to avoid distress in order to cope, a person with BPD may be even more likely to use avoidance behaviors in response to panic attacks. However, as we have discussed before, although avoidance may be effective initially, it is definitely associated with longer-term negative consequences.

**Post-traumatic Stress Disorder**

Finally, post-traumatic stress disorder (PTSD) is also quite common among people with BPD (Lieb, Zanarini, et al. 2004; Zanarini, Frankenburg, et al., "Axis I comorbidity," 2004). In fact, as we mentioned earlier, PTSD is so common among people with BPD that some clinical researchers have suggested that BPD may actually be a form of chronic or lasting PTSD (Herman 1992). Now, most people would disagree with this idea, and it is important to keep in mind that not everyone with BPD has PTSD or has experienced a traumatic life event. However, the simple fact that some people have suggested that these disorders are closely intertwined does highlight the fact that these two disorders often go hand in hand.

So, why do they go hand in hand? Well, as we have discussed, BPD and PTSD are caused by some of the same kinds of experiences. For example, in chapter 3, we described that childhood abuse is one of the types of experiences that may cause BPD. Similarly, childhood abuse is one of the traumatic events that can lead to PTSD. In fact, chronic abuse during childhood is one of the best-known causes of PTSD (Widom 1999; Zlotnick 1997). Therefore, people who are abused during childhood may grow up to have BPD, PTSD, or both.

What's more, there is reason to believe that people who have BPD may actually be more likely to develop PTSD after experiencing a trauma (Axelrod, Morgan, and Southwick 2005). Basically, one of the things that causes PTSD to develop after people have experienced a traumatic event is the use of unhealthy coping strategies, especially when they are dealing with negative emotions. As we have discussed previously, people with BPD generally have difficulties regulating their emotions and, as a result, they tend to use unhealthy strategies to regulate their emotions, like avoidance. So, if someone with BPD experiences some type of trauma when they are an adult (a rape, or a terrible car accident, for example), they may have a tough time coping with the aftermath of this event, and they may resort to unhealthy behaviors like substance use or binge eating to deal with the distress they are experiencing. Unfortunately, though, as we've discussed several times, coping with distress by avoiding it doesn't usually work in the long term, and these types of coping strategies may actually make someone more likely to develop PTSD.

## Summary

Because BPD influences how people feel, think, behave, and interact with others, it probably isn't too surprising that BPD rarely occurs on its own. There are so many problems that go along with having BPD that it's not hard to see why people who struggle with this disorder might also have other disorders. In this chapter, we reviewed the disorders that tend to be the most common among people with BPD, and described some of the reasons why these disorders may go hand in hand with BPD. In general, the disorders that seem to be most common among people with BPD are emotional disorders, such as depression, bipolar disorder, and anxiety disorders, and disorders that involve problems controlling behaviors, such as substance use and eating disorders. Now, if you are someone who has one or more of these disorders in addition to BPD, the good news is that many comprehensive treatments for BPD will actually help treat these other disorders as well. Treatments like DBT (Linehan 1993a, which we will discuss more in chapter 8) actually work to address many of these other symptoms as part of the treatment for BPD. So, although having another disorder on top of your BPD can make recovery more difficult, you will probably not have to get treatment for each of your disorders individually. And, remember, for some disorders like depression, the symptoms of these disorders will probably get better simply as a result of your getting treatment for BPD.

# 6

# Suicidal Behavior and Deliberate Self-Harm

*Randy started hurting himself when he was thirteen years old. It started as a game, when his friend Bill dared him to burn himself with a lighter. At the time, he was really upset about a big fight he had just had with his mom, so he took Bill up on the dare. Strangely enough, the burning made him feel less tense and less worried and angry about the fight. Soon, he started burning himself several times per week, whenever he felt especially sad, ashamed, or angry. Eventually, when he was eighteen, he made his first suicide attempt by overdosing on his antidepressants.*

Suicide and self-harm are big problems for people with BPD. That's why we decided to devote a separate chapter just to these issues. Not only are these behaviors very common among people with BPD, but they are also some of the most serious problems that people with BPD struggle with. Unlike some of the other problems that go along with BPD, self-harm and suicidal behaviors are life threatening and can lead to death. Therefore, it is essential for you to know as much as possible about these behaviors. Later on, in chapters 11 and 12, we describe some skills that may help you deal with thoughts about suicide and cope with your emotions. Here, we give you some information on self-harm and suicidal behaviors, including how they differ from one another and why people sometimes engage in these behaviors.

# What Do Self-Harm and Suicidal Behavior Mean?

This is actually a much more complicated question than it appears to be. Even people who study and treat suicidal and self-harm behaviors don't always agree on what to call them, or how to define them. In this section, we clarify exactly what is meant by terms like *suicide, suicide attempts, suicide gestures,* and *deliberate self-harm,* among others.

## *Suicide Attempts*

A *suicide attempt* is an act in which you deliberately hurt yourself in order to end your life. Hurting yourself without wanting to kill yourself is not a suicide attempt. In order for an act to be called a suicide attempt, it has to be done with the clear intent to cause death.

Although this difference may seem pretty clear, the issue of intending to die has been the source of a lot of confusion. For instance, people sometimes show up at the emergency room after having cut themselves in order to feel better (with no desire to end their lives) and are labeled "suicide attempters." This misunderstanding might lead an ER doctor to try to hospitalize them or put them on a twenty-four-hour psychiatric hold, out of fear that they could kill themselves.

Although this might be a good idea if a person was actually at risk for killing herself or himself, it's not helpful if the person was just trying to get some relief and really does not want to die.

On the flip side, sometimes people harm themselves and really do want to die but are called "self-injurers" and are not taken seriously. In this case, people who are in desperate need of help sometimes do not receive the assistance they need—which can lead to very devastating consequences. Consider, for example, the case of Michael. When Michael had a difficult therapy session one day, he began to cut himself in the restroom afterward. Remembering the safety plan that he and his therapist had come up with, though, he stopped before he went too far and drove himself to the emergency room of a local hospital. He told the doctor, "I need help. I tried to kill myself and I'm still thinking about it." However, the doctor decided that the cut didn't look that bad and that Michael probably just wanted some attention. Not believing that Michael was really at risk for killing himself, the doctor discharged him, and, the next day, Michael committed suicide.

In our experience, there is a big difference between hurting yourself in order to kill yourself and hurting yourself to feel better. Therefore, it is very important for you (and your therapist, if you have one, and even your family members) to know whether you intend to die as a result of harming yourself.

## *Suicide Completion*

The terms *suicide completion, successful suicide,* and just *suicide* refer to the act of actually killing oneself, which is, quite obviously, different from a *suicide attempt.* In many cases, suicide attempts do not actually result in death. We know that this probably seems like an obvious point, but it is important for you to know about all of the terms used to describe these behaviors.

## *Deliberate Self-Harm*

As we mentioned above, hurting yourself without intending to kill yourself is not considered a suicidal behavior. This kind of self-injurious behavior has been given many names, including *self-harm,* *deliberate self-harm,* *nonsuicidal self-harm,* *self-injurious behavior,* and *self-injury.* We have done a lot of research on this kind of behavior, and we prefer the term *deliberate self-harm,* because it expresses the fact that people do these things on purpose.

# *Ambivalent Suicide Attempts*

So far, we have been talking about self-injurious behaviors as if it is always clear whether someone intends to die. But, as you may know if you struggle with these kinds of behaviors, sometimes people are not sure whether they want to die as a result of hurting themselves. In some ways, they might want to kill themselves, and, in other ways, they might not want to die. This state of being pushed and pulled in two different directions (wanting to end your life versus not wanting to end your life) is called *ambivalence.* Ambivalence happens when you want something and don't want it at the same time. If you hurt yourself, and you are ambivalent about causing your death, we would call this an *ambivalent suicide attempt.* It's partly a suicide attempt, because you partly want to die, but it's not a clear and definitive suicide attempt, because you also don't want to die.

## *Suicidal Ideation (Suicidal Thinking)*

Some people think about death and dying a lot but do not think about ending their own lives. For instance, at times, you might think about what it would be like for everyone if you were dead. However, such thoughts should not be mistaken for suicidal ideation. S*uicidal ideation* involves thoughts about deliberately ending your life. These are not just thoughts about death or dying—these are thoughts about actually killing yourself.

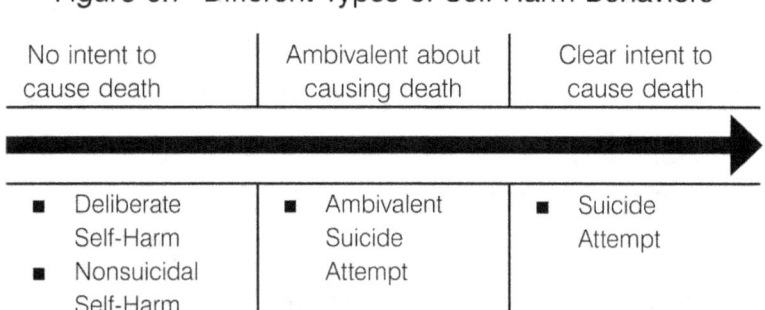

*Figure 6.1* Different Types of Self-Harm Behaviors

# Words and Phrases That We Would Like People to Stop Using

There are a few words and phrases used to describe self-harm and suicidal behaviors that we find troubling. These words and phrases include *suicide gesture, cry for help,* and *manipulative,* among others.

## Suicide Gestures

If you have BPD or have struggled with suicidal behavior, you might have heard this phrase before. Maybe you seriously hurt yourself and someone called it a "suicide gesture." This happens to a lot of people.

Here's the problem with this phrase: the word "gesture" minimizes the seriousness of the behavior as well as the emotional pain of the person who engages in these behaviors. Any kind of intentional self-injury (whether it is a suicide attempt or not) is serious and should not be dismissed. Saying that someone made a "suicide gesture" really means, "He didn't really mean to hurt or kill himself. He was just doing this to get attention."

People use hand gestures to wave, scorn or insult others, and to indicate which line to stand in at the movie theater. Calling a suicide attempt or an act of deliberate self-harm a "gesture" makes it seem like the person only harmed him-or herself to get someone's attention. As we will discuss later in the chapter, most people do not hurt themselves physically to get attention or communicate something to others. And, even if people are desperately in need of some kind of attention from another human being, and have not yet learned any other way of getting that need met, the behavior should not be taken lightly or dismissed.

## Cry for Help

Another similar phrase that is problematic is "a cry for help." Sometimes, after someone attempts suicide or engages in self-harm, other people will say something like "That was just a cry for help." The problem is that, just like *suicide gesture,* this phrase implies that the only reason someone did the behavior was to get other people's attention. It basically ignores all of the other things that lead people to harm themselves or try to kill themselves. In addition, it completely invalidates the emotional pain that usually leads to these kinds of behaviors, and it dismisses the function they serve. Basically, calling these behaviors a cry for help undermines their seriousness and invalidates the needs they meet.

## Manipulative

A third word that people sometimes use to describe self-harm or suicidal behaviors (or the people who engage in these behaviors) is *manipulative.* Far too often, people try to explain away self-harm and suicidal behaviors by saying, "That person was just trying to manipulate me."

There are many problems with using the word "manipulative" to describe these behaviors (or any behavior, for that matter). When you describe someone as manipulative, it is incredibly difficult to feel any compassion or empathy for that person. If you think that someone is just trying to manipulate you, take advantage of you, or get something out of you, you are probably going to be on the defensive and start watching out for your own welfare. You will probably care less about that person and his or her struggles and more about protecting yourself against being manipulated. This, we believe, is a major problem among some people who treat individuals with BPD. How could a therapist maintain empathy, compassion, and understanding while thinking of her or his clients as "manipulative"?

Another problem is that this attitude promotes the idea that we can somehow see inside people's heads and figure out why they are doing things. Even we psychologists don't have that power!

With this attitude comes the assumption that you're doing something on purpose to get something from someone else—that, if you harmed yourself and got attention from a loved one, you harmed yourself on purpose in order to get that attention.

Here's why this kind of thinking is a problem. Oftentimes, we aren't aware of exactly why we do the things we do, or why we keep engaging in the same behaviors again and again. According to the theory behind behavior therapy, people are more likely to engage in a behavior if they get some benefit from the behavior; this benefit is called a *reinforcer* (discussed in chapter 3). The thing is, we are not usually aware of all of the things that reinforce our behaviors. So, let's say a person decides to harm herself because it makes her feel better emotionally. Because it works so well (in the moment), she continues to harm herself whenever she feels really upset. But what if one of the reasons self-harm makes her feel better is that the people around her, including her friends and family, actually pay more attention to her after she hurts herself? This doesn't mean that she was being manipulative, or even that she knows why self-harm helps her feel better. It just means that she is doing what works to meet her needs.

Another problem is that labeling a person as "manipulative" puts the problem inside of that person. If you hurt yourself, and other people pay more attention to you afterward, you may be more likely to continue hurting yourself (even if you are not aware that the care and support you receive is one of the things reinforcing your behavior). If you really think about it, you're not as much the problem in this example as the people who are paying attention to you and reinforcing your behavior. For you to stop hurting yourself, they would have to stop paying attention to you right after you hurt yourself, and you would have to find a better way to get their attention when you are in pain and need support. If people are saying that you're manipulative, it is often true that they have more of a role in your problems than they would like to think.

Finally, as is the case with the other problematic terms we mentioned, the idea that these behaviors are manipulative ignores all of the other reasons people attempt suicide and engage in self-harm. We will discuss this more below, but the number one reason people hurt themselves or attempt to kill themselves is to avoid emotional pain and make themselves feel better. Saying that people who hurt themselves are manipulative dismisses these other reasons.

# The Problem of Self-Harm and Suicidal Behavior in Borderline Personality Disorder

Not only are self-harm and suicidal behaviors incredibly serious, but they are also incredibly common among people with BPD. As we have mentioned before, approximately 1 to 2 percent of the general population has BPD (American Psychiatric Association 2000). However, some studies have found that approximately 10 percent of people who are in outpatient therapy have BPD, and as many as 20 percent of people in inpatient psychiatric hospitals have BPD. What these figures tell us is that people with BPD are overrepresented in psychiatric treatment, and one likely reason for this is the very high rate of suicidal and self-harm behaviors among people with BPD. If you have BPD and have been in the hospital, it's likely that you have made a suicide attempt, seriously harmed yourself, or told someone that you wanted to kill yourself.

## *Some Quick Facts About Suicide and Self-Harm Among People with BPD*

- Around 75 percent of people with BPD say that they have made a suicide attempt at some point in their lives (Frances, Fyer, and Clarkin 1986). This rate is many times higher than the rate for people in the general population and also higher than the rate for people with many other disorders.
- Between 5 and 10 percent of people with BPD actually end up killing

themselves (Frances, Fyer, and Clarkin 1986).
- Some research says that people with BPD make up 7 to 38 percent of all people who end up killing themselves (Linehan et al. 2000).
- Around 69 to 80 percent of people with BPD say that they have deliberately harmed themselves at some point in their lives (Clarkin et al. 1983; Cowdry, Pickar, and Davies 1985; Gunderson 1984; Grove and Tellegen 1991; Stone 1993).
- BPD is the only psychiatric diagnosis in the *DSM-IV-TR* (discussed in chapter 1) that has self-harm and suicidal behavior as one of its criteria.

Now, we don't want you to read this and think, "It's inevitable, I'm doomed. I'm going to kill myself." The suicide rate of 5 to 10 percent means that 90 to 95 percent of people with BPD do *not* end up killing themselves. So, even if you have BPD and have struggled with suicidal behaviors, you have a very high chance of staying alive. If someone were to say, "The chance of rain is 5 to 10 percent," it is not likely that you would be too concerned about wearing a raincoat on your way to work (unless you have a really unreliable weatherperson!). Besides, you can't stop the weather, but there are many ways to stop yourself from committing suicide (see chapter 11). Also, there are some psychological treatments for BPD that are very good at reducing suicide attempts (chapters 8 and 9). So, there is definitely reason to be hopeful.

# Why Do People with BPD Hurt Themselves and Attempt Suicide?

As you read this chapter, you might be wondering why people with BPD are at such high risk for harming themselves. Based on the research, we have a few ideas about why people hurt themselves. Some of the most important and common ones follow.

## *Relief or Escape from Emotional Pain*

A lot of studies have asked people why they harm themselves, and the most common reason that people give is that they were trying to escape or avoid some kind of emotional pain (see Chapman, Gratz, and Brown 2006 for a review). This is true especially for people with BPD. For instance, in one study, women with BPD were asked why they harmed themselves or attempted suicide (Brown, Comtois, and Linehan 2002). Of these women, 96 percent said that they engaged in deliberate self-harm in order to get relief from their emotions; 86 percent said that they had made a suicide attempt in order to get relief from their emotions.

When you think about this, it makes sense. As we have discussed, people with BPD are very emotional. They have intense emotions that may sometimes feel overwhelming or intolerable. At the same time, they have tremendous difficulty managing their emotions, and often they haven't learned how to make themselves feel better when they are upset. If you have BPD, you might have noticed that you have almost no idea how to make yourself feel better when you are really upset. During these times, you might be so overwhelmed by your intense emotions that you start thinking of some way—any way—that you could get some relief. For some people, one of these ways may be deliberate self-harm. Some research has actually shown that people with BPD are more likely than people without BPD to report that they felt better emotionally after they hurt themselves (Chapman and Dixon-Gordon, forthcoming). Other studies have looked at what happens physiologically (or in the body) when people imagine hurting themselves. It turns out that people who have regularly hurt themselves in the past actually show lower emotional arousal when they imagine harming themselves (Haines et al. 1995).

Basically, even though self-harm has a lot of downsides and some pretty serious negative consequences, the fact is that it can make people feel much better in the moment. Although we believe that all of the downsides of self-harm definitely outweigh its short-term benefits, the relief generated by this behavior reinforces it and causes people to rely on it to cope with emotional pain.

So, what about suicide attempts? Why would suicide help you escape from emotional pain? Well, according to one theory, when people experience an upsetting event, they become focused on ways to feel better. In fact, they can become so focused on how they might go about feeling better that they can't do much else (Baumeister 1990; Tice, Bratslavsky, and Baumeister 2001). They might start to have trouble concentrating and thinking clearly, and, in the end, they can get stumped in their quest to find a way to feel better. If they think that nothing will ever work out in the future, they might start thinking that one way to feel better is to commit suicide.

If you have BPD and have struggled with suicidal ideation, this might sound familiar to you. Later on, in chapter 11, we talk about ways to manage thoughts about suicide and to avoid acting on them.

## Self-Punishment

*Sally felt ashamed whenever her boyfriend commented on the fact that she had not had a job for six months. And whenever she felt ashamed she also started to feel angry with herself. She would think, "Why haven't I gotten a job yet? Why am I so lazy? All I do is sit around all day, and do nothing to help myself!" Feeling angry with herself, she would start to think of ways to punish herself for being so "lazy" and "incompetent." One of those ways of punishing herself involved hitting herself in the face.*

Another reason why some people with BPD harm themselves is to punish themselves for some perceived wrongdoing. If you harm yourself, you might relate to Sally and recognize some of your own thoughts and self-talk in that example. Some research has shown that self-punishment is a more common reason for deliberate self-harm than it is for suicide attempts. For instance, in the study where women with BPD were asked why they hurt themselves (Brown, Comtois, and Linehan 2002), 63 percent reported self-punishment as a reason. In contrast, only 38 percent of women with BPD reported self-punishment as a reason for suicide attempts.

It's not clear exactly why people would be more likely to say that they use self-harm (compared with suicide attempts) to punish themselves, but we have some ideas. One possibility is that anger is a very activating, energizing emotion. If you are angry with yourself, you might feel keyed up, agitated, and energized. Anger actually motivates you to do something about your problems, even if what you are doing has some negative consequences. Suicide, on the other hand, is a complete escape from your problems and your life. So, if you are feeling angry with yourself, you might think that you can whip yourself (sometimes, literally!) into shape by punishing yourself, and you might not be thinking as much about ending your life altogether. Another possibility is that you can't really punish yourself if you aren't around to get the punishment. For some people who feel the need to punish themselves, suicide attempts might seem like the easy way out, or too complete of an escape, because they would lose the chance to make themselves suffer.

Now, the problem with self-punishment is that it teaches you absolutely nothing new about solving your problems, and it just makes you feel worse about yourself in the end. In some ways, punishing yourself proves or affirms that you deserved punishment, making you feel even worse. Take the example of Sally above: punishing herself and hitting herself certainly did not help her get a job. In fact, it actually made her feel worse about herself, and then she was even less likely to get herself together to look for work.

Why might self-punishment be an important issue for someone with BPD? Well, remember our discussion about invalidating environments in chapter 3? If you grew up in an invalidating environment, people might have punished, dismissed, or criticized you when you struggled with your emotions. Well, if your caregivers or parents treated you this way, then you might have learned to treat yourself this way. You might also have learned that if you punished yourself first, then they would leave you alone (Chapman, Gratz, and Brown 2006). Unfortunately, this way of dealing with yourself creates more problems than it's worth, and in some cases one of those problems is deliberate self-harm.

## *Generating Feelings*

Some people with BPD struggle with feelings of emptiness and numbness. Others often dissociate, or check out of their surroundings (see chapter 1). So one reason people give for engaging in deliberate self-harm or attempting suicide is to make themselves feel something.

These experiences (dissociation, numbness, emptiness) can be quite uncomfortable, and people with BPD sometimes hurt themselves in order to stop feeling numb and to feel something else in its place, even if it is physical pain. In one study, 54 percent of women with BPD reported engaging in deliberate self-harm as a way to generate feelings, although only 21 percent reported using suicide attempts to generate feelings (Brown, Comtois, and Linehan 2002). So, it seems that generating feelings is a more important reason for deliberate self-harm than it is for suicide attempts. If you really want to generate feelings, killing yourself is probably not the best way to go. If you actually killed yourself, you wouldn't be around to experience whatever feelings that you were hoping to generate.

## *Reducing a Burden on Other People*

Another reason that people with BPD say they sometimes try to harm themselves (especially in the case of suicide attempts) is to reduce the burden carried by other people. If you have BPD, you might sometimes feel like you are a burden to others. You might think that other people would be better off if you didn't have so many problems or were not so emotional. Well, as it turns out, this is a major reason why people say they attempt suicide. In the study of women with BPD mentioned earlier, 31 percent reported making a suicide attempt in order to "make others better off." In contrast, only 7 percent reported that they engaged in deliberate self-harm for this reason. These findings make sense, don't they? If you were thinking of hurting yourself in order to make things better for other people, you would probably think of actually killing yourself rather than harming yourself without dying.

Now, the big problem with this thinking is that, in most cases, people would actually be worse off—*much* worse off—if you were to actually kill yourself. There may be times in your life when this is hard to believe. You might think that you are so much trouble to deal with that people would be relieved if you were to end your life.

But trust us—we have seen what happens to families, friends, coworkers, and even acquaintances when people kill themselves. The survivors are often devastated and take a very long time to recover, if they ever recover at all. In fact, if you kill yourself, your family members, particularly your children (if any), are at much higher risk of killing themselves as well. So, although we can understand why people think this way, it is dangerous thinking—not only for you, but also for the people whom you care about. The people in your life would be *much* worse off if you were to kill yourself.

## Communicating to or Influencing Other People

*Fred had a very hard time telling his partner, Alan, how he felt when Alan went out with other guys. Alan insisted that these men were just friends, and that he simply liked to hang out with different people. He told Fred that he shouldn't be so upset about it and accused him of "pretending" to be upset in order to get attention. Fred felt jealous, hurt, and sad when Alan hung out with other people, but he couldn't seem to find any way to get his feelings across in an effective way. One day, he was so upset that he burned himself. When Alan came home from work, he saw Fred lying on the couch with a serious burn on his arm. He told Fred how worried and sorry he was, and he actually stopped going out with his friends (at least for a few months).*

One final reason for deliberate self-harm and suicide attempts is the need to communicate something to other people. As you can see from the example of Fred and Alan, it can sometimes be very hard to communicate how you feel to someone. You may find that people invalidate your feelings, ignore what you are saying, and have no idea of how much pain you are in. Or, you may not have learned how to express your feelings to other people or share how you are feeling.

People with BPD often struggle with major relationship problems and conflicts. They also have difficulty being assertive or skillfully asking others for what they want. As a result, they might sometimes feel the need to resort to other methods of communication—anything that works to convey how they feel (see the discussion of myth 1 in chapter 2)—and deliberate self-harm or suicide attempts can sometimes serve this purpose. One study found that about 60 percent of people with BPD reported engaging in deliberate self-harm in order to communicate something to other people, and about 45 percent said that they had made a suicide attempt to communicate to others (Brown, Comtois, and Linehan 2002). However, almost all of these people said that they also had other reasons for harming themselves, and that the desire to communicate something, like the extent of their pain, was not the only reason they engaged in the behavior. Instead, communication was one of several reasons. In fact, that's one explanation for why these behaviors are hard to quit—they serve so many different purposes at once!

## *So, What Can You Do About This?*

Knowing why you hurt yourself is often the first step on the way to stopping these behaviors. Now, of course, you might not be at the place in your life where you actually want to stop. Or you might be thinking that stopping would be so hard that you don't even want to try. Indeed, stopping self-harm is probably as hard for some people as it is to quit smoking. But we have seen many people do it. For the moment, let's just assume that you've been hurting yourself or have attempted suicide and you want to stop.

So here's one step that you can take right now. The next time you want to hurt yourself or attempt suicide, just stop and think for a moment. What would you be getting from it? Think about your reasons for hurting yourself or attempting suicide. Then look at table 6.1, below, and ask yourself the questions in this table. You'll see that we have listed the various reasons for hurting yourself or attempting suicide.

If you have different reasons, then use the "other reasons" section.

Next, you'll see some questions to ask yourself before you act on any of your desires to hurt yourself. Basically, these questions get you to think about what you really want and how you can get it without harming yourself. Get a piece of paper and write down everything that comes to mind that does not involve harming or injuring yourself. Then choose one of those things, and do it *instead* of harming yourself.

The more you practice this, the more you will get used to doing life-enhancing things to get your needs met. It can be hard to stop harming yourself, so if you struggle with this, we strongly recommend that you follow our suggestions in the next chapter and start some treatment.

Table 6.1 Some Reasons You Might Be Engaging in Self-Harm and Suicide Attempts and How to Deal with Them

To escape from my emotions or to make myself feel better
- How else can I make myself feel better?
- Can I just ride this out until it goes away?

To feel something—anything
- What else can I do to be able to feel something intensely without causing harm to my body?

To make others better off
- If I feel like a burden on other people, what can I do to reduce this burden?
- Is there anything I can do to take some demands away from the people I care about?

To punish myself
- What am I punishing myself for?
- What would be a better way of reaching my goals?

To communicate to or influence other people
- What do I want to communicate to other people?
- What do I want them to know or understand?

> - What can I do to get the message across without harming myself?
> - Whom can I ask for advice about this? (Choose a really good communicator.)
> 
> Other reasons

## Summary

Self-harm and suicide attempts are common among persons with BPD. If the information in this chapter resonates with you, and you hurt yourself, we suggest that you seek help from someone who has expertise in treating people who self-harm or attempt suicide. See chapter 7 for some advice on how to do this.

Below is a summary of what we have covered in this chapter.

- Suicide attempts involve harming oneself with the intent to die; deliberate self-harm involves harming oneself without the intent to die.
- Suicide and self-harm are commonly occurring problems among people with BPD.

- Problematic terms that people use to describe self-harm and suicidal behavior include *suicide gesture, cry for help,* and *manipulative.*
- The most common reason that people with BPD report for deliberate self-harm and suicide attempts is the wish to escape or get relief from emotions.
- Other common reasons include self-punishment, the need to feel something (or end numbness or dissociation), and a need to communicate to other people.
- If you want to stop harming yourself, think about what you really want, and then find other ways to meet these needs (see table 6.1; also see chapters 11 and 12).

# PART 2
# How Do I Get Help for BPD?

# 7
# How Do I Find Help for Borderline Personality Disorder?

*Mike was beginning to wonder if he had BPD. All his life, he had struggled with his emotions and found himself drawn to intense, stormy, passionate relationships. Although he had wondered for some time if there was something wrong with him, he never knew what it was or how to find out. Recently, though, he had read something on the Internet about BPD, and the description resonated with him. After learning more, he began to think that he might have this disorder. Although much of what he had read seemed pretty hopeful, he wasn't sure where to go from there and how to get the help he needed. He needed a road map for the journey that was ahead of him.*

Thinking that you (or someone you love) may have BPD can bring on a slew of emotions, ranging from fear, to confusion, to hope. Although there is help for BPD, finding this help can be a daunting experience. It is not always clear where to turn or what options are available. In this chapter, we describe how to go about finding help for BPD, the kind of help that is available, and what to keep an eye out for as you figure out the best options for you.

## Treading Safely Through the Minefield: Internet Resources for BPD

The Internet is definitely a mixed bag when it comes to information on BPD. Although some websites are very helpful, providing information on available treatments and cutting-edge research, other websites are replete with misinformation, myths, and bad advice. Making your way through the field of options can be very daunting, and it can be hard to know whom to trust or where to turn. We can help you with this. Below are some websites that we know and trust. These can help you start on your journey toward learning about BPD and finding the help you need.

## *Treatment and Research Advancements National Association for Personality Disorder (TARA NAPD)*

(www.tara4bpd.org)

Founded by Valerie Porr in 1994, this organization is dedicated to helping people with BPD and their family members find accurate information on BPD, as well as available treatment options in their communities. This is one of the most important and influential advocacy organizations dedicated to improving awareness and understanding of BPD. In fact, one of the most important goals of this organization is to reduce the stigma of BPD by (1) making the public more aware of the facts about this disorder and (2) encouraging institutions that fund research (like the National Institute of Mental Health) to provide more money for studies on BPD. TARA NAPD also is dedicated to making effective treatments more available throughout the United States.

The TARA NAPD website is chock-full of useful information for consumers and family members alike (not to mention treatment providers!). One of the most useful services is a nationwide referral program for clinicians and treatment programs offering empirically supported treatments—treatments that have been scientifically shown to be useful. Because they only refer people to treatment providers who use empirically supported treatments, you can be much more confident that you may get a helpful referral from them.

Another great service provided by TARA NAPD is a BPD hotline (1-888-4-TARA APD). In addition to providing treatment referrals for most cities across the nation, this hotline offers educational materials on BPD, edited by experts in this area. Finally, the website provides information on conferences and workshops about BPD, as well as support groups for people with BPD and their families. Many of these meetings are open to the public and can be a great way to learn about BPD and connect with people who are struggling with similar problems.

## *National Education Alliance for BPD(NEA-BPD)*

(www.borderlinepersonalitydisorder.com)

Like TARA NAPD, the NEA-BPD seeks to raise awareness of BPD, providing education on this disorder and promoting research on the causes and treatments of BPD. Led by Dr. Perry Hoffman, the NEA-BPD is one of the foremost leaders in the treatment of family members of people with BPD. In fact, they have developed a twelve-week class that provides information on BPD and teaches skills to family members so they can improve their interactions with their loved ones with BPD. These classes also teach family members coping skills of their own, and they provide access to a support system of people who are dealing with similar problems. These classes, led by family members of people with BPD themselves, are available in cities across the United States and in Canada. The organization's website provides information on classes that are currently available.

The NEA-BPD also hosts several national and regional meetings on BPD each year. Many of the meetings are open to people with BPD and their family members, as well as researchers and clinicians. Typically, these meetings provide information on the newest research on BPD, as well as treatment approaches that are being developed. They generally last two days and are a great opportunity for everyone with an interest in BPD to come together and learn from one another. Information on upcoming meetings is available on their website, along with links to videos of recent talks and workshops—and watching these videos can be a great way of learning more about BPD. Finally, the NEA-BPD also provides reputable information on BPD, including up-to-date research conducted by some of the leading experts in this area.

## The Borderline Sanctuary

(www.mhsanctuary.com/borderline)

This website is a comprehensive resource providing information and education on BPD (including links to clinicians and researchers who work with BPD), chat rooms and online communities for people with BPD and family members of people with BPD, testimonies and personal stories of people with BPD, and treatment referrals.

## BPD Central

(www.bpdcentral.com)

BPD Central is geared primarily toward family members or spouses of someone with BPD. It provides information and educational materials on BPD, and access to a variety of online support groups for family members of people with BPD.

## Behavioral Tech LLC

(www.behavioraltech.org)

Behavioral Tech LLC was founded by Dr. Marsha Linehan in order to train providers to conduct empirically supported treatments such as dialectical behavior therapy (DBT). This website offers a service that provides referrals to DBT treatment providers around the world. In addition, this website offers videos and other materials on DBT skills that can be helpful to people who have BPD (and their families, friends, or therapists).

## Other Ways to Find Information on BPD

These days, the Internet can be one of the best sources of information on BPD—as long as you know where to look and visit reputable and trustworthy websites. However, there are many other ways of finding information on BPD, and many other resources you can use in your quest for help. For example, some people find that it is helpful to read books on BPD. Your local bookstore or library probably has a lot of different books on BPD, including self-help books, autobiographies of people who have struggled with BPD, and reference books written for researchers or therapists.

Depending on what kind of information you are interested in, any of these types of books might be helpful to you.

Another possible way to obtain information is to talk with a local psychology professor. If you are a student (or even if you aren't), professors in the psychology department at your local university might be able to provide you with information on BPD, or recommend therapists in the area who treat patients with BPD. You might also want to go to a community or university mental health center. Places like these often have brochures, handouts, or other educational materials available on a wide range of psychological and psychiatric difficulties. And, even if they don't, someone who works there might be able to recommend another place in your community where you could find the information you're seeking.

An additional way to find information on BPD or get referrals to clinicians or treatment programs is to ask an expert in BPD. Experts in the same fields often know one another. So, if you find the name of someone in your area who conducts research studies on BPD or treats BPD, you could contact that person and ask her or him to refer you to a professional or a treatment program.

# What Kinds of Treatment Are Available for People with BPD?

Generally, two main types of treatments are available for people with BPD: psychological treatments and medication treatments. Psychological treatments normally involve meeting with a mental health professional on a regular basis (such as once per week) and talking about the types of problems you struggle with, figuring out where your problems come from, and working on making the kinds of changes in life that you want to make. In chapters 8 and 9, we are going to tell you a lot more about two particular psychological treatments that have been found to be really helpful for people with BPD; however, keep in mind that there are many other kinds of psychological treatments available that also seem to help (they just haven't been studied as much as the other two).

Medication treatments, on the other hand, normally involve meeting with a psychiatrist, getting an evaluation to determine what type of medication might work for you, and receiving a prescription. You would then meet with the psychiatrist on a regular basis to monitor how you are doing on the medication and any side effects you may be experiencing. (Please see chapter 10 for more details on medication treatments.) Below, we discuss the types of psychological and medication treatments that you might encounter in your efforts to find help.

## *Psychological Treatments*

Depending on where you live, there may be a variety of treatment options available for BPD. Often, these treatments will differ in terms of how intense they are (in other words, how many hours per week they require) and how long they last. Typically, more-intensive treatments have a shorter duration than less-intensive treatments. At the "most intensive" end of the spectrum are inpatient hospitalization programs. These programs provide round-the-clock care and typically involve fairly short stays (sometimes as short as one day, and usually only a few days). Inpatient treatment programs are generally used when people are in a state of crisis, or at serious risk for killing themselves. Most often, the goal of this type of treatment is to help people make it through an immediate crisis.

The downside of inpatient treatment is that it takes people out of their normal lives for a while. And, although getting away from your life might sound like a pretty good thing to you, it can be a problem because it prevents people from really dealing with their difficulties. Because this type of treatment is so intensive, it is usually not recommended for extended periods of time.

Somewhat less intensive is a partial hospitalization program. These programs typically involve several hours of treatment per day, for several days per week. Because people go home at night and are not under direct supervision twenty-four hours per day, these programs are often used to help people make the transition from an inpatient unit to outpatient treatment (which requires fewer hours per week). Partial hospital programs are becoming more popular and are available in many communities. In fact, there are quite a few partial hospital programs that provide specialized treatments for people with BPD.

The least intensive, most common, and best-known type of treatment is outpatient care. For most people, outpatient treatment involves anywhere from one to five hours of treatment per week. Normally, this type of treatment consists of individual therapy for one or two sessions per week, which may be combined with some form of group therapy or participation in a support group. Many different types of individual therapy may be available in your area. Some common types include the following:
- *Cognitive behavioral therapy (CBT).* This kind of treatment helps people learn new skills for managing their

emotions, thoughts, or behaviors. CBT is often a fairly structured form of treatment, with sessions focusing on figuring out patterns that aren't working very well, learning new skills, and changing behaviors that are no longer useful. CBT also often involves homework assignments, where clients practice new skills and change behaviors outside of therapy sessions.
- *Dialectical behavior therapy (DBT).* DBT is a particular form of CBT that combines the elements of CBT that we described above (such as becoming aware of unhelpful patterns, learning new skills, and changing behaviors) with strategies for helping clients learn how to accept themselves, their lives, and other people. We will tell you a lot more about DBT in the next chapter.
- *Psychodynamic therapy.* This kind of treatment helps people figure out why they do the things they do, and where these patterns come from. Psychodynamic therapies focus a lot on people's experiences growing up, helping them to see how past experiences with caregivers and

others influence how people act today. There are actually many different kinds of psychodynamic therapies, ranging from more to less structured and from more to less present-moment focused (in other words, focused on clients' current difficulties as opposed to their past experiences). In general, however, psychodynamic treatments are less structured than CBT and are less likely to involve learning new coping skills and doing homework outside of session.

Although each of these different types of treatments can be helpful, experts on the treatment of BPD often say that it is best to choose the least-intensive treatment possible (Gunderson et al. 2005). Basically, the more that your treatment can be integrated into your real life (and the more time and opportunities you have to live your life!), the better off you are.

## Medication Treatments

In addition to these different types of psychological treatments, certain medications may help alleviate some of the symptoms of BPD. Experts in the treatment of BPD generally agree that it is best to use medication treatments only in combination with psychological treatments, since medications alone don't seem to do the trick (Gunderson 2001). People generally see a psychiatrist for medication treatment, although some primary care physicians will also prescribe psychiatric medications. We'll talk more about medication treatments in chapter 10.

## What to Expect When You Meet with a Mental Health Professional

Many different types of mental health professionals can provide psychological assessments and treatments for BPD, including clinical psychologists (mental health professionals with a Ph.D. or Psy.D. in clinical psychology), psychiatrists (medical doctors with training in the treatment of psychiatric disorders), and social workers (mental health professionals with an MSW or LICSW). All of these types of mental health professionals are trained to provide psychological treatments, and many are trained to provide psychological assessments. However, only psychiatrists are able to provide medication treatments.

**Psychological Assessments**

When you get a thorough psychological assessment, you can expect to be asked a lot of questions about your mood, emotions, thoughts, and problematic behaviors. A lot of the questions will focus on the kinds of symptoms you are dealing with currently, and some will ask about things you may have experienced throughout your life. Typical questions that are used to figure out if someone has BPD include the following:
- Are your relationships stormy or chaotic?

- Do your emotions or moods change a lot?
- Have you ever deliberately hurt yourself without meaning to kill yourself?
- Are you unsure of who you are or what you are really like?

A psychological assessment might also include completing some forms or questionnaires about things like your mood, history (such as childhood abuse), current symptoms, medical history, and current medications.

Now, some people have a lot of difficulty opening up and sharing personal information with someone else—especially someone they have just met. If you have this difficulty, then you might be scared that the person conducting your assessment will judge you, reject you, violate your confidentiality by telling other people about you, or even decide that you are crazy and hospitalize you. We suggest that if you have any of these concerns, you express them to the person you are meeting with. Tell this person what your worries and concerns are. Then, once you have gotten some reassurance, be as open and honest as possible about yourself and your difficulties. The only way you can get help for your problems is if the person you are meeting with has accurate information about what those problems are.

## Individual Therapy

When it comes to individual therapy, the first few sessions often involve a get-to-know-you phase, where you will be asked to talk about the reasons you are seeking treatment, your current problems, how long you have struggled with these problems, and the treatment(s) you have received in the past. Many individual therapists will also be interested in knowing more about your past, including what your early relationships with family and friends were like, what your intimate relationships (if any) have been like, and how you did in school. Your therapist may also want to know more about your family members (including whether they have any mental health problems or diagnoses, and whether they are in treatment).

Once your therapist has learned about your current problems and some of what you have been through in the past (which generally takes a few sessions), she or he will probably want to develop a treatment contract with you—in other words, an agreement about your goals for treatment and the focus of your sessions. Even if you do not create and/or sign a formal agreement or contract, most therapists have a discussion with their clients about their goals for treatment, and the things they would like to accomplish or work toward during therapy. Often, this discussion is intended to make sure that the therapist and client agree on the focus of treatment and have a shared understanding of the treatment goals. Once this agreement is reached, therapy will proceed. As we discussed before, the actual focus of therapy and structure of the sessions will depend on the type of therapy.

**Group Therapy**

Because group therapies are so diverse and have such different goals and purposes, what you will be asked to do in the group and your role as a group member will vary greatly. For example, depending on the particular kind of group therapy you are entering, the way you are introduced to the group may differ. If you are joining a skills-based group that is already under way, you will probably be asked to briefly introduce yourself to the members of the group, and then the group leader will move forward with the material for that day. If you are joining an interpersonal or psychodynamic group, the introductions may be more formal, and you may be asked to provide more information about yourself and why you are joining the group. In this case, the other group members will probably provide a lot more information about themselves as well. Or, if you are starting a new group therapy, with all new members joining the group together, the first session may involve slightly longer introductions from all the members of the group and the group leaders, and a discussion of the rules and guidelines for being in the group.

## Medication Treatments

Although this is not always the case, if you are seeing someone just to get medications (and not for individual therapy as well), you can probably expect that the sessions will be fewer and shorter. Although the first couple of sessions with a psychiatrist (or other professional licensed to prescribe medications) may be longer, and may involve learning more about your current and past symptoms and treatments, later sessions may be only fifteen to thirty minutes. These sessions will probably focus primarily on your current symptoms, any changes in symptoms you have experienced, and any side effects of the medications you have noticed. In general, if you are seeing someone only for medications, the focus of the meetings with this person will be on issues related to the medications, rather than on other problems you may be dealing with—especially if you also have an individual therapist. That being said, most people who provide medication treatments have been trained to provide psychological treatments as well.

Therefore, if you don't have an individual therapist and are seeing someone for medication treatment only, we would still encourage you to ask this person for support when you are struggling and for advice about coping skills that may be helpful for you.

## Specific Steps for Getting Help

We hope you now have a better idea about where to find information on BPD, the types of resources that are out there, and some of the treatments that may be available in your area. Next, let's talk about the exact steps you can take in order to find help.

### *1. Find a Mental Health Professional with Training and Experience in Treating BPD*

The websites we mentioned earlier in this chapter will be a good place to start looking. Many of these websites provide referrals to providers with expertise in the treatment of BPD. If you aren't able to obtain referrals for clinicians in your area, you have several options. For example, you could contact a mental health professional at a local hospital, medical center, or university and ask for a referral. Generally, professionals at places like these will know of reputable clinicians nearby and will be able to provide you with information about treatment programs specializing in the treatment of BPD. Also, some communities have mental health directories that list the services available in particular areas. For instance, in Vancouver, British Columbia, the "Red Book" provides a listing of virtually all mental health service centers in the area. In order to find listings like these, we suggest that you look in your local phone book or get in touch with mental health service providers in your area.

## 2. Get a Thorough Psychological Assessment and Diagnosis

Although reading about BPD in books and on the Internet might help to give you a sense of whether you have this disorder, it is critical that you get a formal diagnosis from a trained professional. Sometimes, when people read a lot about some condition or disorder, they start to see the symptoms in themselves and others—even if those symptoms aren't really there! In fact, this tendency is so common among medical students and interns (who spend a lot of time reading about different disorders and physical illnesses) that there is a name for this phenomenon: medical student syndrome. So, as you are reading about BPD, remember that it's never a good idea to self-diagnose, and that it is really important to get a thorough psychological assessment and formal diagnosis before deciding on a treatment.

## 3. Get Recommendations for Treatment

Usually, once you have met with a professional for a couple of sessions and received a diagnosis, that person will recommend a treatment that may be helpful for your particular difficulties. If you have received an assessment and diagnosis from a practicing psychologist or psychiatrist, that person might offer to provide you with treatment her-or himself. However, the mental health professional who provides your assessment may not provide therapy or may decide that you would be better off seeing a different treatment provider. In that case, this professional would refer you to someone else for treatment. Further, not only will you receive recommendations for individual therapy, but you might also get referred to group therapy (such as a DBT skills group) or to a psychiatrist for medication. When someone provides you with referrals, don't hesitate to ask about the qualifications, experience, and specialties of the treatment providers you are being referred to. In fact, this is so important that it is the next step.

## 4. Ask Questions and Discuss These Recommendations with the Person Giving Them

In order to get the right treatment, you need to make sure that both the person providing the treatment and the treatment approach are a good fit for you. And the only way you will be able to find this out is to get as much information as possible. So, ask as many questions as possible so you can be an informed consumer. Important questions to ask to help you get the best treatment possible include the following:

- What kinds of credentials do you have (or does this program have)? What is your educational background and training? Are you licensed?
- How long have you been treating people with BPD?
- Do you have specialized training or experience in the treatment of BPD?

- What kind of treatment is provided (such as cognitive behavioral, DBT, or psychodynamic)?
- What types of treatment are available (such as individual therapy, group therapy, family therapy, or medications)? Will I have access to more than one type?
- How long does treatment normally last?
- How many hours per week does this treatment involve?
- What will I be expected to do in this treatment (for example, homework, or attending a group)?
- What is the cost of the treatment? Do you accept private insurance, Medicare, or Medicaid?

## 5. Figure Out the Type of Treatment You Would Like to Pursue

Once you have gotten all the information about your available treatment options, it is time to figure out what treatment is the best for you. Getting referrals and recommendations from a trusted source is definitely a good first step, but, in the end, only you can decide which treatment will work best for you. Are you someone who wants a more active, problem-solving approach? If so, maybe cognitive behavioral therapy or DBT would be a better fit for you. Do you prefer to hear from people who are struggling with the same kinds of problems as yours? If so, group therapy might be a really good choice. Next, think about qualities you prefer in a therapist (gender, age, and personality, for example). The answers to all these questions will help you decide which options to choose. However, in the end, the best way to figure out whether a treatment provider is a good fit for you is to meet with that person and let her or him know what you are looking for in therapy. Asking some of the questions that appear in table 7.1 might help you decide whether a particular therapist is right for you.

Think about whether the particular therapy being offered seems like a good approach for you, or whether you would like something else from therapy. If you think you might benefit from a different approach, bring this up to the therapist. It definitely never hurts to ask. Plus, some of your preferences or suggestions may be welcomed by the therapist!

Another thing to consider is how the therapist plans to respond to the particular problems you have. For example, if you struggle with the urge to harm yourself, you are probably going to want to know how the therapist would respond if you hurt yourself while you were in therapy. Although one of the goals of treatment will likely be to help you reduce these dangerous behaviors, let's face facts—you're human and you might slip now and then. Therefore, you'll probably want to make sure that your therapist has a plan for dealing with these behaviors. You might also want to make sure that this person will not kick you out of therapy simply because you slip a couple of times.

Table 7.1 Important Questions to Ask a Mental Health Treatment Provider

- What is the name of the therapy we are going to do?
- What kinds of changes can I expect to see as a result of this treatment?
- Is there any research support for this treatment?
- What are the risks of this treatment?
- How often will we meet?
- How long do you think this therapy will last?
- How do we decide when to stop therapy?
- What is your policy on emergencies?
- Do you take phone calls from clients?
- What should I do if I am having urges to harm myself or kill myself?
- What do you do with clients who hurt themselves or are suicidal?
- What happens when you are on vacation or away for business?

## Summary

The take-home message from this chapter is that help is available if you have BPD, and that there are more and more ways of finding this help. We know that it can be overwhelming to try to figure out where to start and how to go about finding the help you need (or someone you love needs). However, resources are available to guide you as you start down this road. One of the most important things to remember as you try to find the help you need is that you can never have too much (accurate) information. You have a right to information about available treatments and treatment providers, and finding this information will help you make the choices that are best for you. So, ask questions, consider all your options, and pay attention to your gut feelings when it comes to finding the treatment that is right for you.

# 8

# Dialectical Behavior Therapy

*Maria was at the end of her rope. She had been struggling with her emotions for as long as she could remember. Sometimes, Maria couldn't think of any way to cope other than to cut herself, drink a bottle of vodka, or try to end her life altogether. After attempting suicide a couple of times, she ended up in therapy. But she quit after only three sessions, because all she and her therapist did was sit and talk. She had wanted to learn new things and make some changes in her life, and just talking without any kind of focus didn't seem to be helping. So she went to another therapist. This other therapist told her that he wouldn't see her if she kept cutting herself—basically punishing her for having the very problems that had brought her to therapy in the first place. Despite feeling discouraged and hopeless, Maria decided to give therapy one more shot. She had read about something called dialectical behavior therapy and called up a local clinic to make an appointment.*

As we have mentioned throughout this book, if you struggle with BPD, there is hope. There are effective treatments for BPD—treatments that help people learn how to reduce out-of-control behavior, reach their goals, and improve their lives in areas that are important to them. Dialectical Behavior Therapy (DBT; Linehan 1993a) is one of a couple of psychological treatments that have been found to be useful for people with BPD.

# Where Did Dialectical Behavior Therapy Come From?

Back in the 1970s and early 1980s, Dr. Marsha Linehan, a psychologist and professor at the University of Washington, embarked upon a daunting task—she wanted to develop an effective treatment for suicidal women. At the time, very few treatments worked for suicidal people. There was a smattering of evidence showing that some medications could help, and some behavioral treatments also held some promise. But for clients seeking treatment, the situation was much like walking through the desert, never quite knowing where or when the water would show up. For those who were trying to help suicidal people (such as Dr. Linehan), the task was akin to trying to irrigate the desert and grow a lush garden. Fortunately, through a lot of hard work over the past twenty years or so, things have changed.

## Dialectical Behavior Therapy: Finding a Life Worth Living

*Maria told her therapist that she could not stop thinking about killing herself. It used to be that she only thought about suicide when something really stressful happened, like her boyfriend breaking up with her, or losing her job. But, nowadays, it seemed like she thought about suicide even when she was just having an annoying day full of hassles (losing her keys, getting locked out of her car, getting into a small fight with her mother, and so on). Whenever these annoying things happened, she would think, "I could just kill myself and then I wouldn't have to deal with all of this stuff anymore." "The problem," her therapist said, "is that killing yourself is the worst way to improve your life."*

Dr. Linehan's goal was to find a way to help suicidal women develop lives that were worth living. DBT is not a "stop trying to kill yourself" treatment; instead, it involves helping people develop lives that are worth sticking around for (Linehan 1993a). Of course, these goals (having a life worth living and stopping suicidal behavior) go hand in hand. It is hard to want to live if your life is not worth living, and it is hard to develop a life worth living if you are trying to end it.

Being suicidal is a lot like being locked up in a dark room—a room so dark that you can't even see the doors to get out. There are actually several doors in the room; you just can't see them. However, one of the doors has a faint light underneath it. This is the "suicide door." The suicide door is very tempting—it's easier to see than the other doors, and you just happen to have the key to it. So, you spend your time camped out at the suicide door, at times just looking at it and feeling comforted by the idea that there's a way out. You might actually open the door (in other words, you might attempt suicide). The problem is that when you hang out at the suicide door, you can't see the other doors that lead out of the dark room and into a life worth living (Linehan 2005).

There's another problem with walking through the suicide door: you really have no idea what is behind it. Going through that door is like jumping into a swimming pool when you have no idea whether it is full of water or bone-dry concrete. Who knows what you will find if you walk through that door! We really have no idea what happens to people who kill themselves. Some people think that suicide offers peace or an escape from their problems, but what if this is not true? It's a pretty big risk to take. What if you killed yourself because your partner rejected you, only to find out that you were now doomed to an eternity of being rejected by your partner over and over again? Then you'd be in big trouble, because you couldn't kill yourself to get out of being dead!

DBT focuses on helping people with BPD find the other doors out of the dark room and into the light of a life that is fulfilling, enjoyable, rewarding, and—above all else—worth living.

## *The Beginnings of DBT: "Sticky Ideas"*

In developing DBT, Dr. Linehan's objective was to find ways to help suicidal women achieve their goals and reduce their misery. To this end, students and fellow researchers watched Dr. Linehan's therapy sessions and wrote down what seemed to be working well and what seemed to be falling flat. Dr. Linehan also combed through the literature on effective treatments for other psychological problems (such as depression and anxiety disorders). Over time and through a lot of hard work, Dr. Linehan and her colleagues started to knit together a treatment that seemed to be effective for chronically suicidal women. Eventually, she noticed that many of these women met criteria for BPD, and DBT became a treatment specifically for people who struggle with BPD.

Remember our discussion of stigma in chapter 2? Well, before DBT came along, the stigma of BPD was even worse than it is now. People had no idea how to treat clients with BPD. And, one of the things that is most stressful for therapists is to not be able to successfully help their clients. Of course, it didn't help that people with BPD were often perceived as "manipulative" and "angry."

This situation seems to be changing since DBT came on the scene. In his book *The Tipping Point,* Malcolm Gladwell (2000) talks about the fact that there are some ideas in the world that are "sticky" and others that are not. Like the sound of a hammer hitting a large bell, sticky ideas are ones that seem to resonate with people. People find these ideas interesting and remember them. In developing DBT, Dr. Linehan came up with a lot of ideas that seem to be sticking to many of the clinicians, researchers, and clients who have learned about DBT.

Some of the ideas that really seem to resonate with people include the following:

- BPD is a disorder caused by a combination of being born especially emotionally intense and then having those emotions invalidated by others.
- One path out of suffering and misery involves accepting oneself and one's experiences.
- Learning how to develop a life worth living involves figuring out how to manage and tolerate emotions, control behaviors, pay attention to the present moment (practice mindfulness), and navigate relationships with others.

- Therapists must be compassionate and nonjudgmental, and they must balance acceptance of the client with helping the client make important changes in life.
- People with BPD are doing the best they can, and they still have to change (Linehan 1993a).

All of a sudden, therapists who were helping people with BPD had a set of ideas about how to help people with this disorder—ideas that stuck to them like glue and actually made people interested in treating clients with BPD.

# The Theory Behind DBT: The Biosocial Theory

*Maria's therapist started to tell her a little about this treatment called DBT. "The theory is that you were probably always a really emotional person," he told her. "You probably were born like this—just more emotional than most people. When something happens, you react, and when you react, your emotions are very strong and they don't go away easily. The problem is that nobody ever taught you what to do with all of this emotion. In fact, from what you've said, your parents actually ignored you, told you to stop it, or yelled at you whenever you got upset about anything. So, how were you supposed to learn how to deal with your emotions? The problem is that now it's like you're stuck driving a really powerful car, and you can't figure out how to get your foot off the gas."*

Most treatments are based on some kind of theory about what causes the client's problems. Theory is the foundation of the treatment. It explains why certain problems exist and points therapists and clients in the direction of how to fix these problems. In DBT, this theory is called the *biosocial theory* (see figure 8.1). According to the biosocial theory, BPD is caused by both biological factors (being born especially emotionally vulnerable and intense) and social or environmental factors.

*Figure 8.1* The Biosocial Theory of BPD

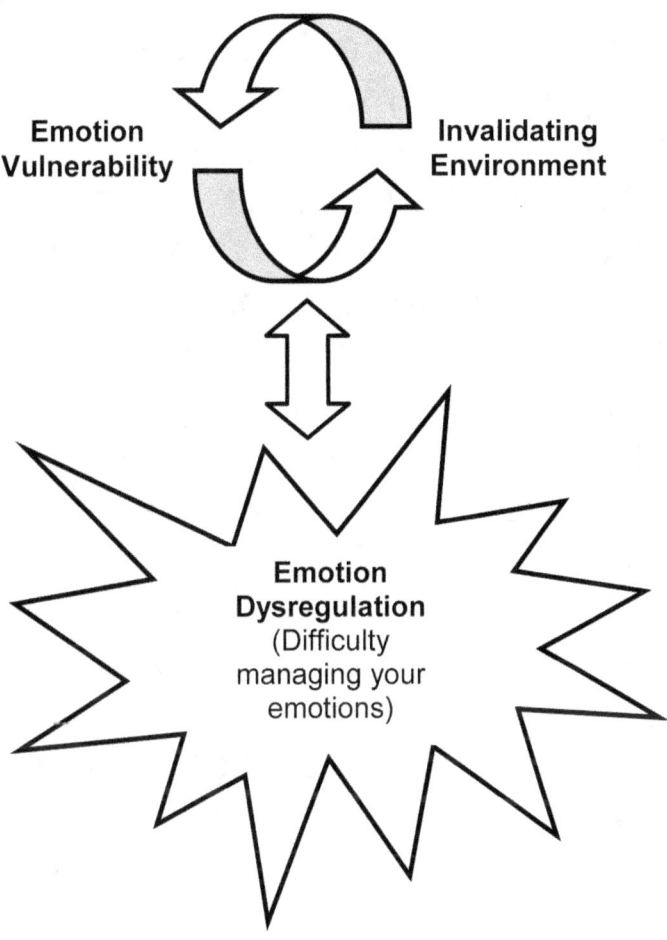

## *Emotion Vulnerability*

*Emotion vulnerability* involves three things: (1) emotional sensitivity, (2) emotional reactivity, and (3) slow return to emotional baseline (Linehan 1993a).

## Emotional Sensitivity

*Emotional sensitivity* is the tendency to have an emotional reaction to events that might not affect other people. For instance, if you are a very sensitive person, it might not take much to make you cry while watching a sad movie or even a commercial on TV. Or, the smallest expression of annoyance from someone close to you might make you feel like you're being stabbed in the gut. Basically, if you are really emotionally sensitive, you are probably going to react to most things going on around you, including relatively small things that less sensitive people might not even notice (a glance, a particular tone of voice, and so on).

## Emotional Reactivity

Being an *emotionally reactive* person means that, when you do react emotionally, you react very strongly, perhaps more strongly than other people do. Basically, you probably have pretty intense emotions. Therefore, not only do you have emotional reactions to many things going on around you (sensitivity), but your reactions are also probably very strong. Have people ever told you that you're really intense? If so, they could be saying that you're emotionally reactive.

**Slow Return to Emotional Baseline**

The third part of being emotionally vulnerable involves having a hard time coming down once you've experienced an emotional reaction. *Slow return to emotional baseline* means that once you feel an emotion (such as anger), it takes a long time for it to go away. For example, if you had an argument with your boss just before you left work and were feeling angry about it, you would most likely still be feeling angry when you arrived home and greeted your partner. Then, if your partner said something that irked you, you would be that much more likely to react with anger or irritation, because you were still feeling angry with your boss.

## *Invalidating Environment*

According to the biosocial theory, people with BPD are not only emotionally vulnerable, but they also grow up in environments where they never learn how to deal with their emotions. Remember that in an invalidating environment, people don't help you learn to deal with your emotions (see chapter 3). Instead, they may tell you that you're wrong for feeling your emotions, or they might punish or ignore you when you get emotional. Now, people do not always say these things in words; sometimes their actions communicate invalidation. Imagine that you are on the bus, and a very heavy person steps on your foot and stays there; you say, "That really hurts," and he says, "Yes, I can see that," but he doesn't do anything to move his foot. This is what sometimes happens in the invalidating environment (Linehan 1993a). Somebody does something that upsets you, you say something about it, but he or she keeps doing it. These are all examples of people in the environment not taking your emotions seriously.

Also, as we have mentioned before, simply growing up in a family where everyone seems different from you can be invalidating. Even if no one is telling you there is something wrong with you,

you may think there is something wrong with you—like you are the "black sheep" or an outsider. It can be really painful to think that you are different or more sensitive than other people are, or that you have a harder time coping with your emotions. Finally, as we discussed in chapter 3, people with BPD often have histories of abuse—physical, emotional, and sexual. These can also be considered parts of an invalidating environment, but it is important to note that even if you haven't been abused, you may still have experienced invalidation from caregivers or others around you.

According to the biosocial theory, people with BPD have had many of these experiences while they were growing up. If you have BPD, you might have also had the experience of people ignoring you, getting angry with you, dismissing you, or rejecting you when you got really emotional. As a result, you may have actually started to be afraid of your own emotions. Keep in mind, though, that the *combination* of emotion vulnerability and environmental invalidation is what leads to BPD. Many people are emotionally vulnerable, but they never develop BPD. Similarly, many people have stressful, invalidating, or even abusive childhoods and never develop BPD. In this theory, "it takes two to tango" so to speak.

It is also important to note that, in this theory, neither factor is to blame. There is nothing wrong with being an emotional person. In fact, there are many advantages to being more emotional. Sometimes, very emotional people are the most interesting, charismatic people in the room. They are passionate about life, they feel others' pain deeply, and they are often very empathetic and sensitive. Similarly, out of no fault of their own, people who are less emotional may not know exactly what to do with a very emotional person, especially a very emotional child. It's as if there's this back and forth between the invalidating environment and the emotional child. The child gets really emotional, and the parents or caregivers don't know how to deal with it. So, the caregivers may tell the child to "stop being so emotional"—not because they want to hurt or upset the child, but simply because they don't know what to do or how to help the child. So, what usually happens when someone tells you not to feel what you're feeling? You're likely to feel it even more! What's more, you're likely to get upset or defensive, or feel out of control. Now you're even more emotional than you were before. And your caregivers now have even less of an idea about what to do, and they may start feeling out of control themselves, or even upset or angry.

Therefore, according to the biosocial theory, both factors are important, and one can amplify the other. Over time, as this happens again and again, emotionally vulnerable people may start to have a lot of difficulty managing their emotions, and they may become afraid of their emotions, find them intolerable, and spend a lot of time trying to avoid them. Indeed, many people with BPD say that they do things like self-harm and suicide attempts in order to escape their emotions (Brown, Comtois, and Linehan 2002). Drug use, binge eating, and other risky behaviors are also used for that same purpose. People with BPD often do these things in order to feel better in the short term, but, of course, all of these behaviors create a whole host of problems in the long term.

## Acceptance, Change, and Dialectics in DBT

As she was developing DBT, Dr. Linehan noticed something very interesting. As we mentioned earlier, one of the first things she did when she was working on this treatment was to comb through the literature and try to apply treatments for other disorders to suicidal women with BPD. These treatments included cognitive behavioral therapy (CBT). CBT is a form of therapy that is very effective for many disorders. In CBT, the therapist helps you to identify and change emotions, thoughts, and behaviors that contribute to your problems. Although CBT seemed to be pretty helpful for many problems, Dr. Linehan also noticed that many of her clients reacted negatively to CBT. They got upset, quit therapy, or didn't show up for their sessions. Although many of them stopped hurting themselves or attempting suicide, they didn't like the treatment and felt invalidated and misunderstood. And it's hard to benefit from treatment when you think your therapist doesn't understand you. So Dr. Linehan began to use strategies to help clients feel more understood and learn how to accept themselves, their lives, and other people (Robins and Chapman 2004).

## *Validation in DBT*

In order to help clients feel more understood, DBT uses *validation.* Validation involves verifying that people are indeed thinking what they say they are thinking, and feeling what they say they are feeling, as well as expressing genuine interest and understanding. DBT therapists always look for opportunities to validate their clients' experiences—to express genuine interest, understanding, and empathy for their clients.

## *Acceptance in DBT*

Through DBT, therapists help clients accept themselves, the world, their emotions and thoughts, and other people by teaching skills such as mindfulness, and techniques for accepting reality for what it is. Now, accepting isn't the same as approving, appreciating, liking, or desiring, and it certainly doesn't mean giving up or surrendering. Accepting is letting go of the struggle to change something and allowing it to be what it is. For example, when you're really upset, you may want to change how you feel. That is perfectly understandable. The problem is that, sometimes, no matter how hard we try, we simply can't change how we feel. In these instances, trying to change your emotions will just make you more distressed.

The same processes are at work when we are having trouble accepting some aspect of our past. Try as we might, we just can't change our history. We can't change the fact that we've done things that we regret, that terrible or traumatic things have happened to us, or that people close to us have died or left us. The more we struggle to change these things, the more upsetting they actually become. So, accepting is all about dropping the struggle to change, and just allowing things to be as they are—at least for now.

Of course, acceptance doesn't mean that you can't change things that actually can be changed. Although you can't change your history or the fact that you get upset, you can find ways to take care of yourself when you get upset, and to work to solve individual problems in your relationships and your life in general (which may help you to feel upset less often).

## *Change and Problem Solving in DBT*

DBT is also a problem-solving treatment that involves pushing clients to change in ways that are very difficult (and yet very necessary). DBT is practical and often focuses on solving problems in your life. If you are suicidal and have BPD, then clearly something needs to change in your life. Having a therapist who doesn't help you to change anything is like asking for directions to Los Angeles and not getting any directions at all. As we discuss below, acceptance with no change is not likely to be helpful, and change with no acceptance doesn't work very well, either.

## What Does Dialectical Mean?

The word *dialectical* is given center stage in DBT because of the emphasis on balancing acceptance and change in treatment (Linehan 1993a). A *dialectic* is the tension between polar opposites—between good and bad, right and wrong, or what you want to do (sit on a beach and drink margaritas, for example) and what you have to do (go to work). It can also be the tension between the need to accept things as they are and the need to change your life. A dialectic is like the rope in a tug-of-war.

Dialectical theory in DBT focuses on the way in which these polar opposites come together and form something that is more complete (Linehan 1993a). For example, many of us struggle to balance the demands of our jobs with the demands of our home life. We want to spend more time with our partners and our children, but we also feel pressured to work long hours and spend less time with our families in order to do well at work. If we were to go completely to the side of our careers and spend all of our time at work, we might excel in our jobs, but our home life would be in shambles. On the other hand, if we were to spend all of our time at home with our families, we'd probably be fired. So, each side (work versus family) is incomplete on its own, because it doesn't get us what we want in life—namely, to do well on both fronts. Dialectics is the way in which we achieve this and other goals by balancing opposites and bringing them together.

As another example, one of the main goals of a DBT therapist is to balance acceptance of the client with the need to help the client to change her or his life. It's as if acceptance and change are in a tug-of-war. If your therapist constantly pushed you to change, you'd probably be fed up, feel invalidated, get angry, and maybe even quit therapy. On the other hand, if all your therapist ever did was tell you how much she understood you, accepted you, and got where you were coming from, your therapy probably wouldn't go anywhere; if you struggle with BPD (especially if you are suicidal), you know that something has to change in order for you to have a life worth living. So, change alone is incomplete because it lacks acceptance, and acceptance alone is incomplete because it lacks change. The therapist's goal in DBT is to balance and bring together acceptance and change in a way that best helps the client.

# So, What Exactly Happens in Dialectical Behavior Therapy?

DBT is a comprehensive treatment for BPD with five key goals, often referred to as the five "functions" of DBT (Chapman and Linehan 2005; Lieb, Zanarini, et al. 2004):
1. Help clients to become more motivated to work toward a life worth living, and to stop engaging

in life-threatening behaviors such as self-harm and suicide attempts
2. Help clients to learn important new skills needed to reach their goals
3. Create a treatment environment that promotes progress and improvement, and help the client structure his or her environment in a way that promotes progress
4. Help therapists stay motivated and skillful in helping their clients
5. Help clients transfer what they learn in therapy to their real lives outside of treatment

In order to help clients accomplish these goals, DBT involves four primary components:
1. Individual therapy
2. Telephone consultation
3. Group skills training
4. Therapist consultation team

## *Individual Therapy*

Individual therapy normally happens once a week for about an hour and mostly focuses on helping you address problems in your life. In DBT, the therapist asks you to complete a form each week, called a Diary Card. On this Diary Card, you keep track of how you feel each day (how miserable you feel, how much joy you feel), along with any urges to engage in self-harm or suicide attempts, any actual incidents of self-harm or attempted suicide, and other things such as whether you are taking your prescription medications properly.

In each session, you bring in the Diary Card, and you and your therapist figure out what to pay the most attention to by creating a *hierarchy of treatment targets.* As we've discussed throughout this book, people with BPD often have many problems in life. If you have BPD, you may struggle with being chronically depressed or stressed out, have difficulties with your relationships or with your job, have panic attacks, engage in suicidal behavior, and so on. Your life may be like a tremendously messy desk that you have to clean. There are little pieces of paper, gum wrappers, pens, pencils, half-eaten apples, old calendars, sticky notes, a broken glass, and other items cluttering up the desk. In fact, it is so messy that you sometimes get overwhelmed just thinking about where to start. Because you can't tackle everything all at once, you need a place to start. Maybe you'll start by picking up the broken glass, so that you don't hurt yourself in the process of cleaning up.

In DBT, the treatment hierarchy tells you and your therapist where to start. And you normally start with the top priority: getting life-threatening behavior under control. *Life-threatening behavior* is any behavior that poses an imminent threat to your life, such as attempting suicide or engaging in self-harm. It could also be behavior that threatens other people's lives, such as homicidal behavior. The bottom line here is that treatment won't help you if you're dead (or for that matter, if you are in prison for killing someone else).

The second most important target in DBT is *therapy-interfering behavior,* which is anything that you or your therapist might do that makes it hard for therapy to progress, or for you to benefit from therapy. Therapy-interfering behavior might involve things like being late to sessions, not attending sessions, not paying attention, yelling at your therapist, or calling your therapist too often. For the therapist, it might involve not paying attention to you, being absentminded or forgetting important things, arriving late, missing sessions, pushing you too hard (or too little) to change, and so on. When therapy-interfering behavior is happening, the therapist and the client talk about it and find ways to fix it.

Finally, the next most important target is anything that might interfere with your ability to have a reasonable quality of life. These might include drug or alcohol problems, depression, unemployment, homelessness, and other such problems. In each session, you and your therapist will spend the most time talking about the highest-priority items. And, in every session, your therapist's role is to help you solve problems in life, stay motivated, and keep moving toward the life you want to have.

## Telephone Consultation

Telephone consultation is an important part of individual therapy. The individual therapist is available in between sessions if you need help, via telephone, e-mail, or whatever communication method works best for you and the therapist. In DBT, therapists take calls primarily in order to reduce suicidal crises, help you learn how to apply a new skill in your daily life, or to resolve any conflicts or difficulties between you and the therapist (Linehan 1993a). But, if you are in DBT, you and your therapist might agree to have calls to help you with other issues as well. You can think of telephone consultation as one way in which the individual therapist helps you to bring therapy into your daily life.

## Skills Training

Skills training is a very important part of DBT. The goal of skills training is to help you learn the skills you need to improve your life and reach your goals. Skills training normally happens in groups of three to twelve clients led by two therapists, and sessions last from 1.5 hours to about 2.5 hours. Normally, the first hour or so involves reviewing "homework" from last session, and the next hour is spent learning new skills. The group is much like a class that you might take at school.

In this way, DBT skills training groups are different from some other therapy groups that you may have joined, such as a process group. In *process groups,* members spend time talking about their emotional reactions to other members in the group, discussing relationships and issues with other members, or talking about their past and how it influences them today, among other topics. In contrast with process groups, DBT groups are much more like classes. They are structured, and you don't spend time talking about your feelings toward other members of the group, your past experiences, or your problem behavior. The group mainly focuses on teaching you important new skills.

So, what skills do you learn? The DBT skills include *mindfulness skills, interpersonal effectiveness skills, emotion regulation skills,* and *distress tolerance skills.* Below is a listing of these skills and a brief description of what they involve:

**Mindfulness Skills**

Mindfulness is the state of being fully awake and paying attention to what is happening in the present moment, or "keeping one's consciousness alive to the present reality" (Hanh 1976, 11). If you do yoga, Pilates, martial arts, or other such activities, you may have had some experience with breathing exercises that involve paying attention to what is happening in the here and now. The following is a list of the types of DBT skills (Linehan 1993b) that fall into the category of mindfulness:
- Paying attention to the present moment without judging it
- Noticing sensations (sights, sounds, smells, tactile sensations) that are happening in the here and now
- Describing "just the facts" of what is happening in the present

- Throwing yourself fully into whatever you are doing right now, in the present
- Focusing on one thing at a time, and doing what works

**Interpersonal Effectiveness Skills**

Interpersonal effectiveness skills are designed to help you manage relationships with other people in an effective manner. As we have mentioned, one of the problems that goes along with BPD is the tendency to have trouble in relationships with others. You might notice that your relationships are stormy, chaotic, unfulfilling, or distressing. You might also notice that you sometimes have trouble asking people for what you want, or saying no to what others ask of you. Interpersonal effectiveness skills are all about navigating relationships effectively. They might include (Linehan 1993b):
- Keeping your goals for your relationships in mind
- Effectively asking others to do things or saying no to others, without being too passive or too aggressive

- Validating other people's feelings, and being honest, truthful, and fair with others

**Emotion Regulation Skills**

Emotion regulation skills are designed to help you manage your emotions in an effective manner. As we have discussed, we believe that one of the major issues in BPD is difficulty managing emotions. You might have noticed that you just don't know what to do when you feel upset, or that, no matter what you do, you can't get yourself to feel any better. Perhaps the things that do make you feel better (such as drugs, self-harm) also cause many other problems. Emotion regulation skills are all about managing your emotions in ways that work for you and don't cause other problems. These skills might include (Linehan 1993b):
- Managing your emotions effectively
- Observing or accepting your emotions
- Changing (increasing or decreasing) your emotional experience
- Making yourself less vulnerable to emotions by increasing pleasant

events in your life, taking care of yourself, and meeting your physical/emotional needs

**Distress Tolerance Skills**

Sometimes, the only thing you can do to get through a tough situation is tolerate it—at least for now. For instance, if someone has put a dent in your car, and you aren't able to get to the mechanic for a week or so, you are probably going to have to tolerate the fact that your car has a dent. If your partner just left you, and you are extremely upset, you might need to tolerate your feelings and the situation until you can find some way to make it better. Distress tolerance skills are all about tolerating and getting through upsetting events, thoughts, and feelings without making things worse. Distress tolerance skills include (Linehan 1993b):

- Getting through difficult situations and feelings without making things worse
- Surviving crises by distracting yourself from painful experiences or making the current moment better or more enjoyable

- Accepting reality for what it is

## *Therapist Consultation Team*

The therapist consultation team is another very important part of DBT. This is a team of therapists who meet, usually once per week, to talk about issues in using DBT to treat clients with BPD. In developing DBT, Dr. Linehan noticed that it can be stressful for therapists to treat clients who are attempting suicide or engaging in other self-destructive behaviors. Although therapists care about their clients and want to do their best to help them, they are human too. It is difficult to see people suffer as much as people with BPD suffer.

If you have BPD, you know what we're talking about. You might have noticed that other people in your life who care about you sometimes have a hard time seeing you in so much pain. So it is very important for therapists to have a way to stay motivated so they can keep doing effective therapy. This is what the therapist consultation team is all about.

The philosophy of the therapist consultation team is that all members of the team are treating all clients on the team. So, every member of the team feels just as responsible for your treatment as your actual therapist does. Therapists help each other stay motivated, act skillfully, and provide effective treatment. The team usually includes therapists who are doing DBT and are seeing clients with BPD or related problems (such as difficulty managing emotions, suicidal behavior, etc.). The team members provide support and encouragement to each other, give each other feedback when their efforts seem to be going astray, and monitor whether team members are getting burned out or using ineffective strategies in therapy. Essentially, the consultation team is like therapy for the therapists. We have been on several of these teams, and we have found that this is one of the most rewarding aspects of doing DBT. In addition, a client often feels reassured that the therapist has a group of people helping her or him provide the best treatment possible.

## The Scientific Evidence for DBT

So, why have we included DBT in this book? It's not just because the ideas are "sticky," or interesting. It's because this treatment works. In order to understand what we mean when we say that the treatment works, you will find it helpful to know how people put together new treatments and test them in the first place.

First, the researcher figures out that there is a need for a new treatment. In the case of DBT, no good treatments for suicidal women existed, so clearly there was a need for a new treatment.

Second, the researcher puts together the ingredients of the new treatment and checks out whether people like it and are willing to do it, rather like a chef trying out a new recipe in his or her restaurant. After seeing how people like it, the chef might decide to change the recipe or perhaps start offering it as a regular feature on the menu.

Developing new treatments is very similar. The researcher first puts together the ingredients of the new treatment, and then he or she gets people to try it out in order to see if they like it and find it acceptable. This is called *feasibility* research. A treatment that is not acceptable or feasible won't go anywhere.

Third, the researcher makes changes based on feedback from clients and on how well the treatment is working so far, and then he or she puts together a manual for the treatment. Then, she or he tests out the manual by conducting controlled experiments called *randomized clinical trials* (RCTs). RCTs are studies where clients are assigned randomly (for example, by flipping a coin) to receive either the new treatment or some other kind of treatment (called a *control treatment).* The control treatment might involve a different intervention, or it might just mean having to wait some time before getting the new treatment. RCTs are the gold standard in research on treatments—the best way to figure out whether a treatment works.

For DBT, so far, there have been eight published RCTs. Most of these studies have included suicidal or self-injurious women with BPD. Also, many of the studies have compared DBT with treatments ordinarily given to people with BPD. For instance, the very first study (Linehan et al. 1991) compared DBT to "treatment as usual" (the kind of treatment that clients with BPD normally got in the community). DBT was better at reducing suicide attempts, self-harm, problems with anger, and hospital and emergency room visits. DBT was also better at increasing clients' social functioning, and it was a lot less expensive than "treatment as usual."

Since this first study, researchers have conducted several other studies of DBT. A recent study (Linehan et al. 2006) compared DBT to other treatment provided by a group of therapists in the community who are considered experts in treating BPD. This study found that DBT was better at reducing the rate of suicide attempts, the medical risk of suicidal and self-harm behavior, hospitalization, anger problems, and the number of dropouts (people who drop therapy). Findings from several other studies have also indicated that DBT is a useful treatment, especially in reducing suicidal behavior, anger, and problems with impulse control, and in increasing social functioning (Robins and Chapman 2004).

Remember our discussion of the baggage (other psychological problems) that comes with BPD? Well, researchers have also tested to see if DBT works for some of these other problems, especially drug use and eating disorders. The research findings are very promising. For instance, some studies (Safer, Telch, and Agras 2001; Telch, Agras, and Linehan 2001) examined DBT for people with binge-eating problems. At the end of treatment, 89 percent of the clients who had been in DBT had stopped binge eating. Other studies have found that DBT is effective at helping people with BPD reduce their drug use (Linehan et al. 1999). In addition, in almost all studies on DBT, the clients report that they feel less depressed and hopeless after treatment.

# So, How Do You Find a Therapist Who Does DBT?

If you are looking for a DBT therapist, the first thing we would suggest is that you go and see a trained professional who can do an assessment to figure out whether you have BPD or the types of problems for which DBT works. If you do, and you wish to see a DBT therapist, one excellent resource is an organization called Behavioral Tech LLC, mentioned in chapter 7. Dr. Linehan founded this organization as a way to help therapists and treatment providers learn how to do DBT. The Behavioral Tech website (www.behavioraltech.org) offers an extensive directory of people who are trained in this treatment.

Other ways to find a DBT therapist include the following: (1) ask a mental health professional in your community whether she or he knows of anyone who does DBT, (2) do an Internet search (type "DBT" and the name of the city in which you live in the "search" field), or (3) contact your state or provincial psychologist association and see if they are aware of anyone who does DBT. These days, many people are aware of DBT and/or have had some training in this treatment. The good news is that professionals no longer think that BPD cannot be treated. There are good treatments out there for BPD, and DBT is one of those treatments.

## Summary

DBT is one of a couple of psychological treatments that have shown great promise in the treatment of BPD. If you want to learn more about DBT, see our reference list for the books by Dr. Linehan (1993a, 1993b) that describe this treatment and the skills that are taught to clients. Below, we summarize the information on DBT that we have included in this chapter.

- DBT was developed by Dr. Marsha Linehan at the University of Washington, originally in an attempt to put together an effective treatment for suicidal women.

- DBT therapists place a lot of importance on accepting and validating clients' experiences, and helping clients to accept themselves, the world, and others.
- DBT is a practical treatment that helps clients solve their life problems and work toward their goals.
- Clients normally see a therapist for weekly individual therapy and attend a skills training group. DBT therapists often belong to a team of other therapists who provide each other with feedback, encouragement, and support.
- Several studies have shown that DBT works for BPD. In fact, DBT is supported by more scientific evidence than any other psychological treatment for BPD.

# 9

# Mentalization-Based Treatment

*Veronica had never been close to her parents. They had always been busy trying to make ends meet, and, even though she appreciated how hard they worked to provide for her, she had never really bonded with them. She often felt as if they didn't really know her and she didn't really know them. This distance between Veronica and her parents also didn't help much when she was trying to manage her emotions and relationships. For Veronica, relationships were one big ball of uncertainty and confusion. She never felt understood and didn't know how to change that. She also never felt like she could read or understand other people. In the midst of all this, her emotions felt overwhelming and out of control. She was desperate for help and didn't know where to turn.*

*That's when she read about mentalization-based treatment and thought it could help.*

In this chapter we look at another treatment that has been shown to help people with BPD: mentalization-based treatment (MBT; Bateman and Fonagy 1999). Now, MBT hasn't been around as long as DBT has, and it hasn't been studied as much either. The first study of MBT was done in the late 1990s (Bateman and Fonagy 1999), and, as of this publication, a second study was expected to be completed in late 2007. So, you probably haven't heard as much about MBT as you have about DBT. However, research that has been done on this treatment has been very promising. In fact, the first study of MBT found results that were similar to results from studies on DBT. And these results tell us that MBT may be very helpful for people with BPD.

# What Exactly Is MBT?

MBT was developed by two clinical researchers in England, Dr. Anthony

Bateman and Dr. Peter Fonagy. And, even though some of the parts of this treatment are similar to DBT, it is based on a very different idea of what BPD is and how it should be treated. As we discussed in chapter 8, DBT is based on the biosocial theory. According to this theory, emotional vulnerability and problems regulating emotions are some of the biggest problems in BPD. MBT is based on a different view of BPD. Instead of focusing on problems with emotions, MBT focuses on people's sense of who they are, or their "sense of self." Basically, MBT is based on the idea that BPD is the result of a *weak self-structure,* or an unstable sense of self and a poor understanding of the self.

Because MBT and DBT are based on such different ideas of what BPD is and how it comes about, it probably won't surprise you that the ways in which these treatments seek to help people are also quite different.

## Type of Treatment

First, MBT is a psychoanalytic treatment, not a cognitive behavioral treatment. What this means is that MBT is more of a "talk therapy" than DBT. In MBT, most of your time is spent talking with your therapist and learning about yourself and your relationships with others, rather than learning new skills and doing lots of homework assignments, as you would in DBT. Although you might walk away from MBT having picked up some of the same new skills you would get in DBT, you would learn those in a more indirect way. Later on in this chapter, we will explain exactly what to expect if you are in MBT.

## Treatment Goals

The second thing that makes MBT different from DBT is the focus of the treatment, or the treatment goals. As you may remember from the last chapter, one of the things that DBT focuses on the most is helping people learn to regulate their emotions in healthy ways, instead of doing things that make their problems worse in the long run (for example, attempting suicide or harming themselves). In contrast, the most important goal in MBT is to increase *mentalization.* Mentalization is the ability to understand that our own behaviors, and the behaviors of people around us, arise from internal mental states such as thoughts, feelings, and desires. Basically, if you have learned how to mentalize, you are able to see that the things you do result from your thoughts, feelings, or desires. These actions don't come out of the blue or occur randomly—they are related to how you feel and the thoughts you have.

One of the main ideas in MBT is that people with BPD have a hard time understanding how their behaviors are related to their mental states. For example, people with BPD might find themselves yelling, or drinking, or hurting themselves and not know why they started doing those things, or what was going on inside them that led to those behaviors. If you have BPD, you might feel like your impulsive behaviors "just happen" or "come out of the blue." Although it can certainly seem that way, that isn't usually what happens. Instead, you might not be aware of the feelings or thoughts you were having before you started acting impulsively, or you might not see the connection between your mental states and your behaviors. The fact that you can't see this connection doesn't mean that it isn't there; it just means that you aren't aware of it. MBT helps you to understand this connection between your mental states and your behaviors.

Of course, just as it is important to be able to understand how your behaviors are related to your mental states, it is also important to be able to understand how other people's behaviors stem from their mental states. For example, let's say that the mother of a teenage boy yelled at him when she learned that he had been driving while intoxicated. Mentalization would allow the boy to understand that his mother was yelling at him because she was scared and angry and wished he would never do it again. If the boy weren't able to mentalize, he might not understand how his mother's yelling was related to her feelings and thoughts.

Mentalization also involves the ability to understand that mental states are related to but separate from behavior. So, for example, it involves being able to understand that the man sitting next to you and crying could be sad, or he might have had his feelings hurt, or he could even be angry. And it also means being able to understand what you yourself are thinking, feeling, and wanting. Does this last piece sound familiar? That's probably because understanding what you are feeling and thinking is also really important in DBT. In fact, this is one area where these treatments are quite alike. Basically, both of these treatments are based on the idea that people with BPD have a hard time figuring out what they are feeling, and how their feelings and thoughts in the moment might lead to a variety of actions (including impulsive behaviors).

# The Theory Behind MBT

Mentalization is usually learned gradually during childhood (Bateman and Fonagy 2004). Children with supportive, caring relationships with their caregivers develop the ability to mentalize during the first few years of their lives by interacting with their caregivers. The basic idea is that children begin to learn what they are thinking and feeling through a process of *mirroring.* So, for example, if a child was with her father and began to cry, he might say, "Oh, are you sad? What happened? Why are you sad?" Because of her father's questions and interest in her feelings, the child would have her emotions mirrored and validated and would learn that crying might indicate sadness. This is a great way for children to begin to learn about their feelings, because it gives them a language for their feelings and also shows them that someone else can understand and respect their feelings. Over time, children can begin to apply this mirroring to themselves and, ideally, can begin to validate and label their own feelings.

Now, because mentalization develops gradually over many years, children often experience two states before they have fully mastered the ability to mentalize. These states represent children's early attempts to understand the relationship between their behaviors and their mental states.

One of these states is *psychic equivalence.* In this state, people believe that other people are just like them and have the same experiences as they do. It's kind of like experiencing the outside world, including other people, as a direct extension of yourself. If you are in a state of psychic equivalence, you might believe that you know everything there is to know about the external world because it is just the same as you are.

For example, let's say that you are deathly afraid of public speaking and have gone to a lecture on some topic. During this lecture, the speaker makes a joke, and only a couple of people in the audience laugh. If you were in a state of psychic equivalence, you might believe that the speaker is now mortified and in a state of panic, just because you would be feeling those things if you were the one up there speaking. The idea that the speaker might not be bothered by the audience's reaction would not even cross your mind because you would be seeing the speaker as equivalent to you (or having the same mental states as you do).

One of the problems with psychic equivalence is that it can be overwhelming, since everything can seem very personal and intense. Think about it—it can be hard enough to live your own life and have your own experiences. Feeling as if you are completely connected to everything around you would probably be quite difficult for most people to deal with.

The second state that people experience before they have fully developed the ability to mentalize is called *pretend mode.* In pretend mode, your mental state is completely disconnected from the external world and from the rest of your mental states. In this state, you might feel really disconnected from yourself, your emotions, and the world around you, and everything might seem unreal. For example, someone in pretend mode might be able to think about what it would feel like to be sad, or even "try on" the feeling of sadness (by pretending to be sad), when she or he was not really feeling that way and there was no connection with reality or the external world. It's sort of like someone talking about feeling sad without actually being in touch with any real feeling of sadness. In fact, at its extreme, pretend mode is basically the same as dissociation. In general, pretend mode can be a very unpleasant and isolating experience.

So how do these two states relate to mentalization? Well, as you may have noticed, these states are opposites, reflecting two different extremes. On one hand, psychic equivalence involves feeling as if the world around you is an extension of you. On the other hand, pretend mode involves feeling cut off or isolated from yourself and the world around you.

In some ways, mentalization balances these two states so that you can better understand yourself and others. With mentalization, people's internal and external worlds are seen as connected to one another but separate. In other words, people understand that their internal states and the outside world are not the same thing, but they also know that they are not completely unrelated. So, if you are able to mentalize, you would understand that your actions (yelling or waving at someone, for example) are related to your feelings and thoughts, that these actions can cause reactions in other people (such as anger or happiness), and that these reactions may then cause these other people to respond in certain ways (yelling back at you or smiling at you, for example).

## *The Development of BPD as Seen Through the Lens of MBT*

So far, we've described how children develop mentalization under good conditions, by interacting with supportive and caring caregivers. The problem is that not all children are raised in ideal conditions and not all children have the opportunity to interact with supportive caregivers, so not all children develop this ability. People learn to understand and describe their internal states by having someone around who consistently reflects back to them what they are thinking and feeling. Therefore, if you don't have someone around you who does that—and does so fairly accurately—it can be very difficult to learn about your own thoughts and feelings.

So, let's imagine that you are a child, and you have come home from school feeling really angry because another child in the school yard threw out your lunch. If your mother were to provide accurate mirroring in this situation, she would tell you that you look angry and ask you what has happened to make you feel that way. This would help you learn about your feelings of anger. On the other hand, if your mother were to laugh at you or say that you looked scared, you would probably be confused and feel misunderstood. And, this would definitely make it harder to learn what anger actually is. In fact, inaccurate mirroring is kind of like the invalidating environment that we talked about in the chapter on DBT. Basically, children learn more about who they are and how they feel if they are around people who reflect their feelings and thoughts back to them in an accurate way. So, as you can see, even though DBT and MBT approach these issues in different ways, both of these treatments are based on the idea that being around caregivers who don't understand how you feel, or who aren't able to validate your feelings and help you understand them, can lead to problems.

So, what happens if your caregivers do not mirror your internal states consistently and accurately when you are growing up? Well, according to MBT, people develop their sense of who they are through these mirroring interactions with their parents or caregivers. Therefore, if your parents or caregivers say that you are feeling or thinking something that you aren't, you might be confused about who you really are. In fact, you might start to develop a sense of who you are that doesn't actually match who you really are. For example, let's say that you are an outgoing person, but you are told over and over again that you are shy and scared around others. If you are told this often enough, you could start to believe that you actually are a shy person, even though you aren't. Basically, because children develop a sense of who they are based in part on what their caregivers reflect back to them, children whose caregivers do not reflect the right things back can end up feeling confused about who they are. As a result, they may have a hard time developing a stable identity or sense of self.

What's more, when you try to develop a sense of self based on inaccurate information, not only will you be confused about who you are but you will also probably feel very disconnected or alienated from yourself. The problem with inaccurate mirroring is that the information being reflected back to you is really less about you and more about the person doing the reflecting. And, if you try to base your sense of who you are on this inaccurate information, the sense of self you end up with is just not going to feel right. It's like trying to squeeze a square peg into a round hole—it just won't work! Anthony Bateman and Peter Fonagy (2004) have used the term the *alien self* to describe the part of the self that is developed on the basis of inaccurate mirroring, because it is so different from who the person really is. What's more, because the alien self often reflects the caregiver's negative image of or negative feelings toward the person (such as frustration), this alien self will be not only different but also disturbing. Because it can be so disturbing, most people are going to want to do everything in their power to get rid of their alien self, and to push it away.

## The Dilemma of the "Alien Self"

Unfortunately, regardless of whether you see the alien self as a part of you and try to keep it inside, or try to get rid of the alien self and push it away, there is no good solution. If your alien self remains inside of you, your sense of self will be disjointed. What's more, because the alien self is really about someone else's feelings and beliefs about you (rather than who you are), it often feels like it is controlled by someone else, which can be a pretty unsettling experience!

On the other hand, if you try to push your alien self out of you and into the external world (through a psychological process called *projection*), you are still not in the clear. Because the alien self contains your caregiver's negative feelings about you, pushing it into the external world means that the external world will now have negative feelings toward you. Basically, people who try to get rid of this part of themselves by pushing it outside of them set themselves up for experiencing the external world as angry, hostile, and threatening—another upsetting experience.

## *Mentalization and BPD*

So, how does all of this relate to BPD? Well, Dr. Bateman and Dr. Fonagy (2004) believe that BPD is caused by a failure to develop mentalization, which leads to problems with the person's sense of self (specifically, a weak self-structure). It's these problems with the self that lead to many of the symptoms of BPD. According to MBT, people with BPD are not able to mentalize when they are in a state of emotional arousal, or really upset. During these times, they must resort to other ways of making sense of themselves and others. Specifically, because people with BPD are not able to mentalize during times of intense distress, they rely on the use of psychic equivalence and pretend mode to maintain some sense of self during stressful times. In fact, many of the impulsive behaviors that people with BPD often struggle with are thought to be a desperate attempt to protect the self and deal with the alien self in some way.

    For example, people with BPD may become overwhelmed by the negative and harsh alien self inside of them. Because having an alien self is so awful, a person with BPD may harm her-or himself in an effort to punish or destroy this alien self (and develop a stronger or more cohesive sense of self). Alternatively, someone with BPD might try to get rid of the alien self by pushing it outside, into the external world (where it is often seen as being part of someone else). In this case, the person with BPD might lash out at this other individual in an attempt to destroy the alien self once and for all. According to MBT, this is one of the primary reasons why people with BPD have such stormy relationships.

## So, What Can I Expect in MBT?

MBT is a comprehensive treatment that was first developed as a partial hospital program. As we described in chapter 7, the number of hours per week spent in treatment in a partial hospital program falls somewhere between inpatient hospital programs and standard outpatient therapy. The MBT partial hospital program involves six hours per week of structured treatment, including one hour of individual therapy, three hour-long sessions of group therapy, one hour of expressive therapy, and a community meeting.

Although the only published studies as of summer 2007 had focused on this partial hospital program, at press time Dr. Bateman and Dr. Fonagy were completing a study that looked at how well MBT works as an outpatient treatment program—which would be far more practical for the vast majority of people with BPD. In this new outpatient form of MBT, clients receive one individual therapy session and one group therapy session per week, for a weekly total of two and a half hours of treatment.

## *Individual Therapy*

If you are participating in MBT individual therapy, you might expect your therapist to try really hard to get you to think about why you do the things you do, and how others might react to those actions. For example, your therapist might ask you to think about how she or he would feel about something you did, and then to reflect upon how these thoughts and feelings might lead to different actions. Your therapist might also spend time thinking and talking about how your behaviors stem from your thoughts, feelings, and desires. All in all, an MBT therapist is going to work with you to help you understand that everyone's behaviors stem from or are related to some internal experience, like thoughts, feelings, or desires.

Your therapist will also probably spend a lot of time trying to understand how your actions relate to your thoughts and feelings, and how your thoughts and feelings relate to her or his actions in therapy. The idea is that your therapist's efforts to understand the ways in which your actions are related to the actions of other people (and to your feelings and thoughts about their actions) will help you to understand these relationships as well. In other words, you might learn how to mentalize. For example, let's say your therapist is trying to understand how your crying in session is related to something she or he just said, and to your feelings of sadness and fear about this statement. According to the principles of MBT, your therapist's efforts to understand these connections will help you start to learn how your actions (in this case, crying) are linked to the things that happen around you, and to your reactions to these things.

It is also worth mentioning that, as in DBT, MBT therapists are encouraged to apply the therapy techniques to themselves. Basically, MBT therapists are taught to consider how their own reactions and behaviors in the session are related to their mental states and the client's behaviors. In this way, MBT therapists are expected to do exactly what they are teaching their clients to do, so the goal of mentalization is present for everyone. This really adds to the sense that you and your therapist are in a collaborative relationship and working together, which is a really important thing to have in therapy.

Finally, keep in mind that both you and your therapist are going to spend a lot of time wondering and being curious about how actions and mental states are related, instead of assuming that either one of you has all the answers or completely understands what the other person is experiencing. This is called taking a position of "not knowing," and it is considered to be important for helping clients develop mentalization.

## What About Group Therapy?

We have been talking about the types of things you might expect in MBT individual therapy. Because MBT is focused on increasing mentalization, you will notice many of these things in group therapy as well. In some ways, you can think about MBT group therapy as the same as MBT individual therapy—just with more people in the room! As we discussed above, in MBT group therapy, all members of the group (and the group leader) are going to take a position of "not knowing" and will try their best to understand how group members' behaviors are related to the behaviors of other members of the group, as well as to their own feelings, thoughts, and desires. In particular, all members of an MBT group would be encouraged to consider the mental states of the other group members, as well as their own mental states. For example, clients would be asked to consider why they think another group member feels the way she does, or why she is acting a particular way. Because of the focus on mentalization (which really involves thinking about other people in relation to ourselves), group therapy actually provides a great opportunity to practice this skill.

# The Scientific Evidence for MBT

So, why have we included MBT in this book? Well, just like DBT, MBT has been shown to help people with BPD. As we mentioned above, the only published study on MBT was done on the eighteen-month-long partial hospital program. In this study (a randomized controlled trial), Dr. Bateman and Dr. Fonagy (1999) compared MBT to the typical treatment clients normally received in the community. They found that MBT was better at reducing suicide attempts, self-harm, and depression and anxiety. What's more, clients who were treated with MBT were still doing better in these areas eighteen months after the treatment had ended (Bateman and Fonagy 2001). MBT was also better at helping clients with their social interactions and relationships, leading to better interpersonal and social functioning overall. Additionally, MBT was better at helping to lessen psychiatric symptoms in general and, like DBT, was better at keeping clients out of the hospital. Best of all, these improvements in social functioning, relationships, and psychiatric symptoms actually continued to grow after the treatment had ended, with the clients who had received MBT showing even more improvements in these areas during the eighteen months after they ended the treatment. The fact that the clients who had been treated with MBT kept improving after the treatment ended is really important, because it tells us that this treatment actually helped clients change in meaningful ways. And what we really want when it comes to psychological treatments is for clients to learn and grow so much that at some point they don't need the treatment anymore.

## Summary

MBT is a psychoanalytic treatment that was developed in England by Dr. Anthony Bateman and Dr. Peter Fonagy. Although MBT was originally developed to be a partial hospital program, it has been turned into an outpatient treatment. The study on this outpatient form of MBT is expected to be completed in summer 2007, but there is definitely reason to be hopeful. Although MBT hasn't been studied as much as DBT has, the existing studies show that MBT helps people with BPD, even after they leave treatment!

Just like DBT, the outpatient form of MBT includes one individual therapy session and one group therapy session per week. In general, the main focus of MBT is on increasing mentalization and helping clients understand that everyone's behaviors stem from or are related to some internal experience, like thoughts, feelings, or desires. Because it is a psychoanalytic treatment rather than a cognitive behavioral treatment, MBT is more of a "talk therapy" than DBT and won't involve as much hands-on skills training. However, in the end, you would probably get some of the same benefits from MBT as you would from DBT. Also, even though MBT isn't as widely available as DBT is, we believe that it is going to become more readily available in the near future, and that it may be a very good treatment option for people with BPD.

# 10

# Medication Treatments

*Joan was sick of her endless mood swings, irritability, and agitation, and she was desperate to find something that would help her. She had recently stopped using alcohol and drugs to cope with her emotions, but now she had no idea what to do to help herself feel better. She went to her physician, who said that she might want to set up an appointment with a psychiatrist. The psychiatrist told her that she had borderline personality disorder. "The thing about BPD is that there is no single medication out there that will solve your problems," she said. "We do know that some medications can help with some of the symptoms of BPD, but right now, there's no 'anti-BPD' medication like there is for depression. Before we get to the specifics, tell me—how do you feel about the idea of being on medication?"*

Many people with BPD try medications—sometimes several medications all at once. If you are a very emotionally intense person, you might have wondered whether some kind of medication could help even out your emotions, or make you feel calmer or more at peace. Or, you might have seen television commercials about medications that help with depression or anxiety and wondered whether these medications could also help you.

This chapter is all about medication treatments for BPD. We discuss different medications that are sometimes used to treat BPD, and some of the evidence for and against these medications. We also talk about some of the things you might want to consider if you are thinking about taking medications, such as your preferences regarding medication treatments, medication side effects, and how to get evaluated for possible medication treatment.

## How Do Medications Work?

So far, we have talked in depth about *psychological* (often called behavioral, cognitive, cognitive behavioral, psychodynamic, or psychoanalytic) treatments, which therapists use to help people improve the quality of their lives by talking with them, helping them change their behaviors, thoughts, and emotions, teaching them new coping skills, or helping them to resolve issues from their past. *Medication* treatments differ from psychological treatments in that they are intended to help people improve the quality of their lives by changing aspects of their body or brain chemistry.

## *Neurotransmitters and Changing Your Brain Chemistry*

As you may have guessed, psychopharmacological treatments are based on the idea that some psychological issues stem from problems in your brain functioning and/or chemistry. For instance, some people believe that problems with the serotonin system of the brain might cause depression. *Serotonin* is a *neurotransmitter,* a chemical in your brain that controls mood, hunger, temperature, sexual activity, sleep, and aggression, among other things.

How does this work? Imagine that there are two houses right across from one another on a narrow street: Sally's house and John's house. These houses are like *neurons,* or brain cells. The street in between the houses is like the *synapse*—the space in between two neurons. Now, imagine that there are dozens of people coming out of Sally's house, milling around, talking with each other, and heading for John's house. When some of these people enter John's house, they turn on the lights, the oven, and the furnace, and John's house becomes active. These people are like neurotransmitters. The more people there are hanging around in the street, the more likely it is that one of them will go into John's house, just to get out of the crowded street, and turn on the lights. Similarly, the more neurotransmitters there are in between two neurons (in the synapse), the more likely it is that they will activate a neuron.

Now, low activity in a house (a neuron) could be due to many things: (1) there are not enough people coming out of Sally's house (not enough neurotransmitters available), (2) the people who come out of Sally's house do not go into John's house (the neurotransmitters do not "bind" with the other neuron), or (3) the people who come out of Sally's house walk around and then go back inside before ever reaching John's house (the neurotransmitters go back where they came from—a process called *reuptake*—before they have a chance to act). Many of the medications used to treat depression tackle the problem of neurotransmitters being taken back into the original neuron (Sally's house) before they can bind with and activate another neuron (John's house). In order for the serotonin system to work properly and ward off depression, serotonin needs to flow freely from one neuron to another. When this doesn't happen, activity in the serotonin system reduces, and one possible consequence is depression. Medications that tackle this problem are called *selective serotonin reuptake inhibitors* (SSRIs), because they prevent some serotonin from being gathered up and taken back into the original neuron.

Other medications work by decreasing the activity of certain neurotransmitters. For instance, some people believe that certain psychiatric disorders (such as schizophrenia) are related to too much activity in the dopamine areas of the brain. *Dopamine* is a neurotransmitter that is involved in mood, the experience of pleasure, and the regulation of body movement. Medications used to treat schizophrenia often block dopamine activity, by blocking receptors for dopamine. For example, these medications would lock up John's house nice and tight, to make sure that nobody named Dopamine got in. Better yet, this would be like having a large bodyguard standing at the door of John's house and preventing all people named Dopamine from entering and turning on the lights. Blocking dopamine receptors prevents dopamine from binding to those receptors and activating the neuron (or turning on the lights in John's house).

## *How Do We Know Whether a Medication Works?*

This, as you might have guessed, is a very complicated question. Before we can say that a particular type of medication is helpful for people with BPD, we have to think about the studies that have been done on these medications. You may be thinking, "Oh, great. Now we're getting to the really boring part!" Well, we would disagree. We believe it is incredibly important for you to know what to make of all the things people say about treatments—medication or otherwise—and figure out whether they are really true.

**How Do People Study Medications?**

In order for you to know what to make of all the claims about medications and how well they work, you have to know about the different ways that people study medication treatments. There are too many to discuss in depth here, but we are going to highlight the two most common approaches to studying medications.

One type of study is an *open-label trial,* a research study in which the experimenters and the patients both know which drugs the patients are receiving. Quite often, researchers use open-label trials when they are first trying out a new medication, or if they are trying to see if existing medications work for different types of problems. These studies are cheaper and easier to conduct than are more sophisticated studies, and they can give a basic idea of whether it makes sense to try the medication in a larger, well-controlled study. The big problem with open-label trials is that patients might get better simply because they *expect* to get better from the medication—a phenomenon called the *placebo effect.* Or, the researchers might expect the patients to get better, and so they might be biased, or they might give subtle hints to the patients that they are better off than they actually are. So, if someone does a study of Prozac and finds that it helps people with depression, this could be due to several different things: (1) Prozac may be helpful in treating depression, (2) patients may have expected to get better, so they got better, or (3) researcher bias may have influenced the findings.

The second main type of study is called a *double-blind, placebo-controlled trial*—a study in which patients are assigned randomly to take either the drug (such as Prozac) or a placebo (such as a sugar pill). These studies are called "double-blind" studies because neither the patient nor the experimenter knows which substance (placebo or Prozac) the patient is taking. Double-blind, placebo-controlled trials are generally more reliable, because they basically get rid of the possibility that the placebo effect could explain the findings—if the active drug does better than the placebo, then this is probably due to the chemical effects of the active drug, rather than a placebo effect. So, as you read the rest of this chapter, and when you look into different medication options (which we encourage you to do), pay attention to what kinds of studies were used to test out the medication(s).

## What Type of Patients Do the Studies Include, and How Many?

Another important thing you should consider is whether the patients in these studies are similar to you. As you'll see, studies are often done on very specific types of patients. For instance, many of the studies on antipsychotic medications (often used to treat disorders like schizophrenia) for BPD have only included people who have psychotic symptoms, such as hallucinations and delusions. So, even if these medications are helpful for those patients, they may not be helpful for you if you do not have those kinds of symptoms. Hence, it is important to know the types of patients and symptoms that the medications work best for. Finally, you might want to be a little skeptical about studies that include very small numbers of patients (for example, less than twenty or thirty). If a study includes a very small number of patients, the effects of the medication on these patients may not tell us very much about what you would find if you used the medication yourself. Generally, including a small number of patients in a study makes it harder to draw conclusions about the effects of a medication for a larger range of patients. With these points in mind, let's talk about some of the medications that are commonly used to treat BPD and whether they actually work.

# Different Medications and How Well They Work for BPD

Generally, the most common medications used for BPD include antidepressant medications, mood-stabilizing medications, and antipsychotic medications. Within this section, we discuss these different types of medications, including how they work and what types of side effects they have. We also give you some information about the use of these medications for BPD.

## *Antidepressant Medications*

Antidepressants are among the most common medications used to treat BPD. *Antidepressants* is the name for a large category of medications that are, not surprisingly, used to treat depression. For the most part, people use antidepressants to treat BPD because they assume that the depression symptoms and emotional difficulties common among people with BPD are the result of problems with the neurotransmitters serotonin (discussed earlier) and/or norepinephrine. *Norepinephrine* (sometimes called "noradrenaline") is a neurotransmitter as well as a hormone. It is involved in alertness, concentration, aggressiveness, motivation, and the fight-or-flight system. The general idea is that people who are depressed do not have enough activity in their norepinephrine or serotonin systems; thus, most antidepressant medications work by increasing activity in these areas.

There are several different types of antidepressant medications. These different types of antidepressants work in different ways, which we will explain below. Generally, these medications fall into four categories: tricyclic antidepressants, selective serotonin reuptake inhibitors, monoamine oxidase inhibitors, and novel antidepressants. As you read the next sections, you'll see that we have included some of the names of common antidepressants. The names in parentheses at the end of each section are the brand names (e.g., Prozac) that you are probably most familiar with. One thing that is very important to remember about these medications is that they sometimes take a while to kick in and start helping with your mood. Often, it takes two to four weeks for antidepressants to start to really work. So, remember that if you are considering these medications.

## Tricyclic Antidepressants (TCAs)

Tricyclic antidepressants (TCAs) work primarily by blocking the reuptake of norepinephrine and serotonin. This means that more norepinephrine and serotonin are available in the synapse and, as a result, these neurotransmitters have a better chance of activating another neuron. This is similar to the situation with John's and Sally's houses. Let's say that a bunch of people come out of Sally's house and are headed toward John's house. But, Sally's family members decide that they want to hang out with these people some more, and so they go outside and try to gather the people back before they reach John's house. A similar scenario happens with neurotransmitters: they get released into the synapse, but after a while they sometimes get taken back into the neuron that they came from before they can reach the nearby neuron and cause it to fire. TCAs prevent this process of *reuptake* (being taken back into the neuron) for both serotonin and norepinephrine. As a result, there is more norepinephrine and serotonin available, making it more likely that these neurotransmitters will cause activity in certain neurons.

As with any medication, it is important to know what side effects to expect with TCAs. Some of the common side effects of TCAs include the following: dry mouth, fatigue, urinary retention, dizziness, blurred vision, hand tremor, constipation, and nausea.

Some common examples of TCAs include amitriptyline (Elavil), desipramine (Norpramin), imipramine (Tofranil), nortriptyline (Aventyl), and clomipramine (Anafranil).

## Selective Serotonin Reuptake Inhibitors (SSRIs)

Selective serotonin reuptake inhibitors (SSRIs), such as Prozac, work in a manner that is similar to that of TCAs. Like TCAs, SSRIs prevent the reuptake of serotonin. This means that they prevent serotonin from being taken back into the neuron it came from before it has a chance to activate another neuron (called the postsynaptic neuron). The difference is that TCAs prevent the reuptake of both serotonin and norepinephrine, whereas SSRIs prevent the reuptake of serotonin only.

Although the side effects of SSRIs often are quite mild, they are common. Some of these side effects include nausea, diarrhea, headaches, anxiety, nervousness, sleep disturbance, restlessness and agitation, fatigue, dizziness, light-headedness, sexual problems (including lower sex drive), tremor, dry mouth, sweating, mania for people who struggle with bipolar disorder, weight loss or weight gain, rashes, and seizures.

Some common examples of SSRIs include fluoxetine (Prozac), sertraline (Zoloft), fluvoxamine (Luvox), citalopram (Celexa), escitalopram (Lexapro), and paroxetine (Paxil).

## Monoamine Oxidase Inhibitors (MAOIs)

Monoamine oxidase inhibitors (MAOIs) work in a way that's a little different from TCAs and SSRIs. As we discussed earlier, the neurotransmitters that seem to be most related to depression are serotonin and norepinephrine. These neurotransmitters fall into a category called *monoamine neurotransmitters.* When monoamine neurotransmitters are released into the synapse (the space between two neurons), they only have a certain amount of time before chemicals in the synapse break them down and they are no longer able to bind to and fire the other neuron (in other words, go into John's house and turn on his lights). One of the key chemicals that breaks down these neurotransmitters is called *monoamine oxidase.* So, the MAOIs inhibit or reduce the quantity of monoamine oxidase in the synapse. As a result, norepinephrine and serotonin are not broken down as quickly, and there is a greater chance that these neurotransmitters will make it to the other neuron and fire it.

It is very important for you to know about the side effects of the MAOIs, because they can be more serious than those of some other antidepressants. Some common side effects include dizziness and cardiac changes, stomach upset, dry mouth, constipation, and headaches. Some of the more severe side effects occur if you consume foods or beverages that contain an amino acid called *tyramine.* Consuming such foods and beverages can lead to an acute *hypertensive crisis* (in which your blood pressure rises quickly, and you may experience the following symptoms: a throbbing headache, heart palpitations, neck soreness, paleness, chills, nausea, vomiting, restlessness, chest pain, fever, and in some cases, stroke, coma, or even death).

It is incredibly important that you follow your physician's dietary recommendations if you are taking an MAOI. You'll need to avoid certain foods and beverages, such as beer, ale, certain types of wine, banana peels, bean curd, fava bean pods, certain cheeses, certain meats, certain types of fish (especially smoked fish), ginseng, protein supplements, sauerkraut, certain soups, yeast, and shrimp paste, among other foods and beverages.

Some examples of common MAOIs include phenelzine (Nardil), tranylcypromine (Parnate), isocarboxazid (Marplan), and selegiline (Eldepryl).

**Novel Antidepressants**

In addition to the antidepressants we have discussed already, several newer medications are being used to treat depression these days. These medications work in a variety of different ways. Your physician or psychiatrist will be able to explain these medications to you.

Some examples of these medications include venlafaxine (Effexor), nefazodone (Serzone), trazodone (Desyrel), mirtazapine (Remeron), and bupropion (Wellbutrin).

## How Well Do Antidepressants Work for BPD?

Most of the studies on antidepressants for BPD have focused on SSRIs (Paris 2005; Silk, Wolf, and Ben-Ami 2005). This is probably because these medications seem to have fewer or less-serious side effects than TCAs or MAOIs. Four open-label studies have indicated good effects of fluoxetine (Prozac) on patients with BPD. In one of these studies, patients who took Prozac had reductions in their sensitivity to rejection, as well as improvements in anger, depressed mood, mood instability (or mood swings), anxiety, and impulsivity (Norden 1989).

A few other open-label studies found that Prozac helped to reduce psychiatric symptoms, depression, anxiety, and interpersonal sensitivity among patients with BPD (Cornelius et al. 1990; Markovitz, Calabrese, and Meltzer 1991; Markovitz and Wagner 1995). A few double-blind, placebo-controlled studies have also found beneficial effects of SSRIs in patients with BPD. For instance, one study found that anger, anxiety, and depression in patients with BPD who took Prozac improved more than they did in patients with BPD who took a placebo (Salzman et al. 1995). Another study looked at how well Prozac worked for patients who had BPD and a mood or anxiety disorder. This study found that patients who took Prozac had greater improvements in depression, anxiety, and other psychiatric symptoms (Markovitz 1995). A double-blind placebo study of another SSRI (fluvoxamine, or Luvox) for women with BPD found that the patients who took Luvox reported more relief from rapid mood shifts, compared to the patients who took placebos (Rinne et al. 2002).

So, given these studies, what can we conclude? Well, right now, the best conclusion we can make is that SSRI antidepressants may be helpful in reducing depression, anxiety, and mood shifts among patients with BPD.

## Can Antidepressants Make You Suicidal?

You may have heard about the recent controversy concerning SSRIs and the concern that these types of antidepressants might increase a person's risk for suicide and suicide attempts. Obviously, this is not a side effect you want if you are trying to find help for BPD! Because of these concerns, the Food and Drug Administration of the United States has asked drug companies to report *risk ratios* for clinical trials—the ratio of risk for suicide attempts or "suicide-related events" for patients taking the medication, compared to the risk for suicide-related events for patients taking the placebo. (Generally, a risk ratio of 1.0 indicates that people taking the active medication have the same risk for suicidal behaviors as patients taking the placebo. A risk ratio higher than 1.0 indicates that patients taking the medication are at higher risk for suicidal behaviors than patients taking the placebo.) Studies of Prozac have consistently reported risk ratios close to or below 1.0 (Whittington et al. 2004), indicating that the risk of suicidal behavior for people taking Prozac is similar to the risk found for people taking a placebo.

However, researchers recently reviewed several studies of different types of antidepressants and found evidence that antidepressant prescriptions were linked to suicidal behavior within the first nine days after patients got the prescription (Jick, Kaye, and Jick 2004; Silk, Wolf, and Ben-Ami 2005). There are no published studies on this topic specifically focused on people with BPD.

Once again, what does this tell us? Well, the best conclusion we can draw based on the studies to date is that for some patients (although not all) antidepressant use may increase the risk of suicidal behavior. Why might this be the case? Although there are many possible reasons, two stand out in particular. First, antidepressants take some time to start working. Patients who start taking an antidepressant and are looking for a quick change in their mood might feel discouraged and hopeless when this change doesn't happen as quickly as they had hoped. In fact, this could explain the finding that the risk of suicidal behavior is highest in the nine days after patients get a prescription for an antidepressant. Second, as people start to feel a bit better (but not completely better), they have more energy, which makes it easier for them to carry out plans to kill themselves. However, we really don't know exactly why there seems to be a link between antidepressants and the risk for suicidal behaviors in some patients. It is important to remember that any time you start taking medications, you should discuss any concerns you have about these medications or your reactions to them with your physician immediately.

## *Mood-Stabilizing Medications*

Mood-stabilizing medications are another type of medication commonly used to treat BPD. When you think about it, this makes sense. If having an unstable mood is a key symptom of BPD, then you might expect mood-stabilizing medications to be helpful. In this section, we will talk about whether this seems to be true. First, though, it is important to know a few facts about mood-stabilizing medications. There are two main types of mood stabilizers: lithium carbonate and anticonvulsants.

**Lithium Carbonate**

Lithium carbonate has been around for some time and is most often used to treat bipolar disorder (see chapter 5 for a description of bipolar disorder). Often referred to as lithium, this medication tends to have a stabilizing effect on people's moods. If your mood fluctuates between very high and very low, you might find that lithium evens things out and makes your mood swings less extreme. Some people who take lithium don't like it for this very reason—they actually like the big mood shifts, and, in particular, the strong highs, which lithium tends to lessen.

It is not clear exactly how lithium works to stabilize moods, but we do know that it is a salt. This means that it can alter your balance between electrolytes and fluids. As a result, you have to be careful about how much sodium you eat and how much fluid you drink if you are on lithium. Some of the common side effects of lithium include nausea, hand tremor, increased urination, diarrhea, upset stomach, increased thirst, and decreased appetite. You should know that lithium has the potential to be very toxic. Therefore, it is important that you work with your psychiatrist to find the dosage that is right for you and do not deviate from that dosage unless your doctor tells you to. Some side effects that could indicate toxic or dangerous effects include slurred speech, increased hand tremor, sluggishness, ringing in the ears, vomiting, uncertain gait, confusion, blurred vision, and excessive thirst.

## Anticonvulsants

Anticonvulsants were originally used to treat seizure-related disorders, but researchers and clinicians discovered that these medications also have a mood-stabilizing effect. Because of this, anticonvulsants are sometimes used to treat people who have problems with mood instability, such as those with bipolar disorder and, sometimes, with BPD. There are several different types of anticonvulsants, and it is not exactly clear how they work. Some research suggests that these drugs work by increasing the activity of a neurotransmitter called GABA.

GABA is an *inhibitory neurotransmitter.* This means that it slows down or inhibits activity in certain areas of the brain. Let's say that Gabe, one of the folks headed to John's house, was like GABA. Whenever he gets to John's house, he immediately finds the circuit breakers and turns off all of the electricity. This is roughly what happens with GABA; GABA inhibits the activity of certain neurons.

Another idea about how anticonvulsants work is that they block the action of *glutamate*—an excitatory neurotransmitter. The opposite of GABA, glutamate would be like the person who turns *on* the electricity in John's house.

Anticonvulsants would handcuff this person to keep her or him from turning on the power. Blocking glutamate prevents activity in certain areas of the brain. The idea here is that by increasing the activity of GABA and blocking the activity of glutamate, anticonvulsants reduce activity in the areas of the brain related to mood swings, and as a result, the person's moods are evened out.

A few common side effects of anticonvulsants include irritability, hair loss, reduced platelet count (which leads to easy bruising), liver toxicity, pancreatitis (inflammation of the pancreas), and possibly polycystic ovarian syndrome (a condition that can influence a woman's menstrual cycle, hormones, fertility, insulin production, cardiac functioning, and appearance). It is also important to know that some of these types of medications (such as divalproex sodium, or DVP) have *teratogenic effects,* meaning that they can do harm to a fetus. Pregnant women should be cautious and should discuss their medication options with their physicians.

Some common examples of these medications include carba-mazepine (Tegretol), oxcarbazepine (Trileptal), valproate/divalproex (Depakote), lamotrigine (Lamictal), topiramate (Topamax), gabapentin (Neurontin), and divalproex sodium.

## How Well Do Mood Stabilizers Work for BPD?

There is some evidence that mood stabilizers may be helpful for people with BPD (Paris 2005; Silk, Wolf, and Ben-Ami 2005). For instance, there is a small amount of evidence that lithium can be helpful for patients with BPD (Links et al. 1990). The problem with this research is that most studies on mood stabilizers have been openlabel trials or have included a very small number of patients. Also, the medication that has been studied the most is DVP. Although DVP has fewer side effects than some of the other mood stabilizers do, it is important to remember that DVP can be harmful to a fetus, so it isn't a good choice for everyone.

A limited number of studies have shown some good effects of DVP for people with BPD. One open-label study of eleven patients with BPD found that after taking DVP for eight weeks, patients had less irritability and psychiatric symptoms (Stein et al. 1995). A larger open-label study of DVP with thirty hospitalized patients with BPD also found that DVP seemed to help lessen psychiatric symptoms (Wilcox 1995). However, double-blind, placebo-controlled studies haven't always had the same good findings. For instance, one study found that DVP was no better than a placebo (Hollander et al. 2001). However, another study that looked at BPD patients who also had bipolar II disorder (Frankenburg and Zanarini 2002) found that patients who took DVP experienced greater improvements in interpersonal sensitivity, anger, and hostility than did the patients who received the placebo.

The best conclusion we can draw is that mood-stabilizing medications may be helpful for some patients with BPD, especially in alleviating irritability, anger, and general psychiatric symptoms.

## Antipsychotic Medications

Sometimes people use *antipsychotic medications* in the treatment of BPD. These medications help treat psychotic symptoms and were originally used with people with disorders like schizophrenia. However, the fact that these medications are sometimes also used to help people with BPD does not mean that those with BPD are psychotic. *Psychosis* is a term for problems with being out of touch with reality. People who have psychotic symptoms might hallucinate (see, hear, feel, smell, or taste things that are not there), have delusions (unusual or bizarre thoughts), or experience other such symptoms. On the other hand, even though BPD is not a psychotic disorder like schizophrenia, people with BPD sometimes do have unusual thoughts or beliefs that they just can't seem to give up (like believing you are ugly or fat, no matter how often people tell you that is not true, and try to convince you otherwise). Therefore, some of the medications used to treat psychosis may be helpful for people with BPD.

Some of the common side effects of antipsychotic medications include sedation/fatigue, low blood pressure, weight gain, temperature increases or decreases (for example, feeling hot a lot of the time), changes in the activity of your heart or cardiovascular system, and changes in your skin pigmentation, among other effects. It is also important to know that some specific medications require special care, such as clozapine. If you are taking this medication, you need to have your white blood cells monitored regularly. Some of the more severe effects of antipsychotic medications include involuntary movements in your face and other body parts (called *tardive dyskinesia),* and *neuroleptic malignant syndrome* (NMS; includes muscular rigidity, elevated temperature, blood pressure increases or decreases, and a sense of altered consciousness). If you have any of these symptoms, it is important that you see your doctor immediately.

There are two main types of antipsychotic medications: *first-generation antipsychotics* and *second-generation antipsychotics.*

Firstgeneration antipsychotics are not used very often for BPD these days, because of their side effects.

Some common examples of *second-generation* antipsychotics include loxapine (Loxitane), clozapine (Clozaril), risperidone (Risperdal), olanzapine (Zyprexa), and sertindole (Serlect).

So how do antipsychotic medications work? Well, there are many theories, but the most common explanation is that they block activity of dopamine areas in the brain. As we have mentioned, *dopamine* is involved in mood, pleasure, and body movement. Problems in the dopamine system (including low activity and degeneration or breakdown of dopamine neurons in certain areas of the brain) can lead to Parkinson's disease. Some people also think that too much dopamine activity might lead to some of the symptoms that people with schizophrenia experience, such as delusions and hallucinations. Although there are differences between the antipsychotic medications, most of them block dopamine receptors (as if a large bodyguard is standing at the door of

John's house and preventing anyone from coming in and turning on the electricity). When the dopamine receptor is blocked, dopamine can't bind with the receptor or cause the neuron to fire.

## How Well Do Antipsychotic Medications Work for BPD?

There is some evidence that antipsychotic medications may be helpful for people with BPD (Paris 2005; Silk, Wolf, and Ben-Ami 2005). Clozapine is one of these, and several open-label studies have examined its effects. One study of fifteen patients with both BPD and a psychotic disorder found that clozapine was helpful in reducing psychotic symptoms and improving social functioning (Frankenburg and Zanarini 1993). Another study of clozapine for BPD patients with major depression and psychotic symptoms found that this medication was helpful in improving psychotic symptoms, depression, impulsivity, and mood instability (Benedetti et al. 1998). Another study found that clozapine was helpful in reducing self-harm behaviors among BPD patients with psychotic symptoms (Chengappa et al. 1999).

One thing to keep in mind, though, is that all of these studies have included patients with BPD who also have psychotic symptoms (Silk, Wolf, and Ben-Ami 2005). So, it is hard to tell whether clozapine would be helpful for persons with BPD who do not suffer from psychotic symptoms. It could be that the improvements of the BPD patients in these studies were due to the fact that their psychotic symptoms got better. In addition, many patients in these studies reported significant side effects, including a lot of weight gain (Silk, Wolf, and Ben-Ami 2005).

Another medication that studies have looked at is olanzapine. One open-label study of olanzapine found that BPD patients with *dysthymic disorder* (similar to depression but less intense and longer lasting) had improvements in many different psychiatric symptoms, except aggression. A double-blind, placebo-controlled study of olanzapine for BPD patients without depression, bipolar disorder, or a psychotic disorder found that BPD symptoms in patients who took olanzapine improved more than in patients who took a placebo (Zanarini and Frankenburg 2001). Another study had similar results (Bogenschutz and Nurnberg 2004).

A third antipsychotic medication used to treat BPD is risperidone. The findings of studies have been mixed for risperidone, however. One open-label study (Rocca et al. 2002) found that in patients who took risperidone, psychiatric symptoms, hostility, and aggression improved. However, a double-blind, placebo-controlled study found that BPD patients on risperidone did not do any better than patients on a placebo (Schulz et al. 1999).

The conclusions we can draw from all of these studies is that antipsychotic medications, especially clozapine and olanzapine, may help with some of the symptoms of BPD. We don't know whether clozapine helps people with BPD who do not also have psychotic symptoms, but we do know that many antipsychotic medications have pretty significant side effects (such as weight gain).

## So, Does Medication Work for BPD?

As you can see, the answer to this question depends on what types of problems you have and what type of medication you're talking about. Although clinicians used to think that it was best to use different types of medications to help with the different kinds of symptoms of BPD (for example, antidepressants and mood stabilizers to manage emotional instability, antipsychotics to reduce cognitive problems, and so on), this no longer seems to be the case (Silk, Wolf, and Ben-Ami 2005). With all of the research out there on medication treatments for BPD, it seems clear that different types of medications can have very similar effects. Most of these medications, even if they were developed to help with very different kinds of problems, seem to have some effect on emotional instability, anger, and other psychiatric symptoms, whether they are mood stabilizers, antipsychotics, or antidepressants. This seems odd when you really think about it, right? You'd probably expect antipsychotics to help with psychotic features and antidepressants to help with mood symptoms. Well, as you can see, psychopharmacology is not an exact science. Drugs that have very different effects on your brain chemistry can actually have very similar effects on the emotional problems people may struggle with.

So, that brings us back to the question, Does medication work for BPD? Well, the safest conclusion seems to be that some medications help with some BPD-related problems, but so far there is no "anti-BPD" medication. As Dr. Joel Paris, one of the leading researchers on BPD, pointed out in a recent article (2005), medications can help treat some of the problems related to BPD, but they are unlikely to lead to complete recovery from this disorder. Many experts would recommend that if you have BPD and are on medication, you should also get involved in some kind of psychological treatment, in order to get the maximum benefits from your medical care.

# Is Medication the Right Type of Treatment for You?

If you have BPD (or think you may have BPD) and are looking for some kind of treatment, you might ask yourself whether you would actually like to be on medication. In our experience, some of the people we see for therapy prefer to take medications to help with some of their symptoms; others would like to avoid medications at all costs. In this section, we discuss some of the issues you might want to consider regarding taking medications. We also discuss the types of questions you should ask your psychiatrist or physician about medications.

---

Table 10.1 Important Questions to Ask About Medications to Ask About Medications

Questions about your prescriber's training and experience:
- What is your experience and training in providing medication treatments to people who have BPD?

- How many patients with BPD have you seen?
- Do you have any formal training in the treatment of BPD?

Questions about how well the medication works:
- How do your patients do on this medication?
- Does this medication work for people with my problems?
- How many people get better on this medication?
- What are the chances that this medication will help me with my problems?
- What can I do, if anything, to make the medication more likely to work for me?
- How long will it take for me to notice a difference?
- How does the medication work?

Questions about things to watch out for:
- What is likely to happen if or when I go off the medication?
- What are the side effects of the medication?

- Which side effects are common, and which ones are rare?
- What types of side effects do I need to be concerned about? (What kinds of side effects might tell me that there is an emergency?)
- Are there any foods or drugs (including alcohol) that I need to avoid if I am on this medication?

Questions about how treatment will go:

- How often will we meet?
- How long will our meetings be?
- Are you available in case of an emergency? If so, how do I reach you and at what hours?
- How will we figure out how well the medication is working?
- What will we do if this medication doesn't work? Will we stop this medication and try another one, or will we keep this medication and add another one?

## *Taking Charge of Your Treatment: Getting*

## Information About Medication

We suggest that before you decide to start taking a medication, you gather as much information as possible. Reading this chapter is a good first step, but don't stop here. Talk with your psychiatrist or physician about the medication options available to you and the advantages and disadvantages of different medications. In table 10.1, we list a number of questions you should ask your treatment provider if you are thinking about starting a medication.

## Deciding Whether to Take Medications

After you have gathered all of the relevant information, think through the pros and cons of taking the medication. Quite often, if you meet with a physician or psychiatrist, you will leave a very brief appointment with a prescription in hand. You may be headed to the pharmacy before you have had a chance to really give some thought to this type of treatment. You may also feel so desperate for help that you are willing to try the first thing that comes along. Instead, sit down and give some thought to this decision before making your choice, just like you will think through your decisions about psychological treatments. Below are some general considerations that might help you decide whether medication is right for you:

- The pros and cons of medication treatments
- The availability of someone in your community who can provide competent medication treatment/management (that is, someone with the necessary experience and expertise)
- The fit of certain medications with your lifestyle, eating patterns, use of alcohol, etc.
- Problems with relapse after medications are terminated
- Cost of medications, and whether they are covered under your insurance/medical plan
- The consequences if you miss a dose

- How long it takes for the medication to work
- The side effects of the medications, and whether you are okay with having those side effects

Come up with a list of pros and cons of medications (see table 10.2 for an example). In the pros category, put all of the positive things that might come from being on the medication. For example, in this category, you might write things like the following: "Improving my mood, feeling less unstable, feeling like I can cope with life better." In the cons category, write all of the negative things that might be related to taking the medication, such as "Chance of significant weight gain (a side effect), other undesirable side effects, possibly having to stay on the medication for a long time." Then, look at your lists and decide whether you want to go ahead with taking the medication. Whatever you decide, make sure that you inform your physician or psychiatrist about your choice.

Table 10.2 Pros and Cons of Medication Treatment

| Examples of Pros of Going on the Medication | Examples of Cons of Going on the Medication |
|---|---|
| • I might feel better. | • It's expensive and my insurance doesn't cover it. |
| • It might improve my mood. | • I would have to avoid certain foods. |
| • I might be able to function better at work. | • I might have to stay on the medication for a long time. |

# *Taking Charge of Your Treatment: Figure Out whether It Is Working*

We also suggest that you and your prescribing physician come up with some way of monitoring whether the medication is working. Often, people who take medications have periodic checkup appointments with their psychiatrists or physicians. These appointments often last for fifteen minutes to an hour or so. They may involve a brief review of the symptoms and side effects that you have been experiencing, a discussion about psychological therapy, advice or assistance in coping with problems in life, or all of these things. But if you are meeting with your psychiatrist or physician only once a month, how are you supposed to remember what your life has been like over the past thirty days and communicate this to your treatment provider in just a brief appointment? Many of us have trouble remembering what happened to us last week, much less several weeks ago!

So, given how hard it can be to remember this stuff, we suggest that one way to help keep track of the emotions, thoughts, behaviors, and symptoms that are important to you is to use a self-monitoring log. You can see an example of such a log in table 10.3. On this form, you can see some of the difficulties that many people with BPD struggle with (such as suicidal thoughts, self-harm, impulsive behaviors, emotional pain). Now, if this form seems like a good fit for you, feel free to use it as is to keep track of the symptoms and problems you are hoping to change. If it doesn't quite seem to capture the problems you are struggling with the most, feel free to change it to make it more useful for you. If you do decide to use this form, we suggest that you start using it before you begin taking a medication, even a couple of weeks before you start, just so you can get a sense of what things are like for you when you are not on the medication.

Make note of the date you started the medication (and what medication it was), and then continue keeping track of your experiences. We also suggest that you fill out the form at pretty much the same time every day. Pick a time that works for you to do this, mark it on your calendar, day planner, or electronic organizer, and start taking charge of your recovery process.

### Table 10.3 Symptom Monitoring Log

*Instructions:*

Use this log to keep track of your symptoms or experiences and to communicate how you are doing to the person who prescribes your medication. You can also use this log to keep track of how you do when your medication changes, or when you don't take your medication as you are supposed to. You might modify this log according to your own specific symptoms or problems. For instance, if you don't struggle with self-harm or suicidal thoughts, then you might put something else in those columns.

Fill this out at the end of the day, every day, so that the information is still fresh in your mind when you note it on the log. For the columns that include 0 to 5 ratings, 0 means none (no emotional distress, self-harm urges, and so on), and 5 means the highest possible level (highest possible emotional distress, self-harm urges, and the like). For the columns that include Yes/No ratings, write "Yes" if the event happened (if you did engage in impulsive behavior, for example), and "No" if the event did not happen.

*Table 10.3* Symptom Monitoring Log *(continued)*

| Day | Emotional Distress | Impulsive Behavior | Self-Harm Urges | Suicidal Thoughts | Self-Harm | Took Meds as Prescribed | Side Effects | Medication Change |
|---|---|---|---|---|---|---|---|---|
| | 0–5 | Yes or No | 0–5 | 0–5 | Yes or No | Yes or No | 0–5 | Yes or No |
| Mon | | | | | | | | |
| Tues | | | | | | | | |
| Wed | | | | | | | | |
| Thurs | | | | | | | | |
| Fri | | | | | | | | |
| Sat | | | | | | | | |
| Sun | | | | | | | | |

Notes (about side effects, symptoms, or other experiences that are important to remember):

## Summary

We hope that you have found this chapter to be helpful and informative. We have covered a lot of information, so below we offer a brief summary of some of the most important points we talked about:
- Neurotransmitters are chemicals in your brain that affect the activity of brain cells (neurons).
- Medications change the activity of your neurotransmitters.
- In trying to figure out whether a medication is helpful, we are most confident about findings of studies that use double-blind, placebo-controlled trials, and that include patients who actually have BPD.
- The medications most commonly used to treat BPD include antidepressants, mood stabilizers, and antipsychotic medications.
- Each type of medication has side effects, and some side effects are more serious than others.
- Antidepressants, mood stabilizers, and antipsychotics have all shown modest

but important benefits for people with BPD, but there is no "anti-BPD" drug yet.
- It is important for you to take charge of your treatment by seeking information on medications, thinking through your decision to take or not take medications, and working with your prescribing physician to monitor how well the medication is working for you.

# 11

# Dealing with Suicidal Thoughts

*Alice was at the end of her rope. She had just gotten fired from her job, and when she came home, hoping to relax and get some support, she found her boyfriend in bed with another woman. Alice felt absolutely crushed and betrayed. After a few days had passed, and her boyfriend had moved out, Alice was sitting in her living room, feeling terribly alone, and thinking about everything she would have to do to get another job and make sure she didn't end up financially destitute. She felt sad and alone, and started to think that life was hopeless and that nothing was ever going to get better. She then started to think about killing herself.*

If you've come with us this far in the book, you've probably been wondering what you can do to deal with your problems. We've talked about what BPD is all about, the types of problems that go along with having BPD, how to get treatment, and what types of treatments are out there. But, even if you are hoping to get treatment soon, it is important for you to know about some of the things that you can do to help yourself manage your emotions, deal with stress in your life, and cope with some of the BPD-related problems.

We included this chapter here because, to be honest, if you kill yourself, the rest of these skills won't work! The most important thing you can do to help yourself cope with your problems is stay alive. The same goes for treatment—if you're not alive to show up for treatment, it won't work for you. And, as we discussed in chapter 6, suicidal thoughts are pretty common for many people with BPD. If you find yourself thinking about suicide, you may be in a lot of pain a lot of the time. In fact, you might be thinking that ending your life would provide a way out of that pain. If this thought process sounds familiar to you, let's assume that, all things being equal, you would rather stay alive and learn to have a less painful life than end up dead. Keep this in mind as we talk about these skills. Also, keep in mind that thinking about suicide and attempting suicide can actually make your life more painful and more difficult. So, the goal here is to help you learn to deal with suicidal thoughts (and not act on them) when they come up.

## Steps to Take If You Are Feeling Suicidal

If you think about suicide regularly, it may be very hard for you to break this habit. It's as if your brain gets used to thinking of suicide whenever a big enough problem comes through the door. You might actually find it soothing to think about suicide, like you have an escape valve that you can use if things ever get too hard or if you lose hope. In fact, for some people, thinking about suicide can actually become sort of like a reflex—something bad happens, and Bam! Your mind immediately thinks of suicide. Of course, it can be very difficult to change a reflex like this. Sometimes, the thoughts are simply going to come too quickly for you to be able to stop them. So, don't expect that if you use these skills you will never again think about suicide. That might not happen. But what might happen is that you will learn how not to act on your thoughts and you will feel as if you have more freedom to choose what you do. Below, we describe the steps you can take if you are having suicidal thoughts and considering killing yourself.

## *Get Away from "Lethal Means"*

When you are thinking about suicide, one of the very first things you should do is get away from *lethal means*—anything that you could use to kill yourself. People who think about suicide a lot usually have a relatively clear idea of what they would do to kill themselves. If you know what you would do, then be sure to remove yourself from those lethal means immediately. The idea here is that you

are far less likely to attempt suicide if you don't have access to the tools or methods you would use to do the job. Below are some ways to keep yourself out of harm's way:
- If you want to overdose on your medications, then get out of your home and away from your medications, flush them down the toilet (you can always get more later), give them to someone else for safekeeping until the crisis has passed, or lock them up somewhere it would be hard for you to get them on the spur of the moment.
- If you want to harm yourself with a knife or other sharp object, get these objects out of your home, or get yourself away from them.
- Don't let yourself buy things that you would use to harm yourself.
- Don't let yourself "accidentally" drive past the store where you could purchase razor blades or medications. Don't "accidentally" end up at your drug dealer's home where you could buy drugs for an overdose.

## Think About What You Really Want

When you have thoughts about suicide, we suggest that you first think about what you really want. Do you actually want to be dead, or do you want to feel better or get rid of some problem that is bothering you? Dr. Marsha Linehan (Behavioral Tech LLC 2004) has said in one of her videos on DBT, "If you are thinking of suicide that means there's a problem." Most people with BPD say that they attempt suicide in order to escape their emotions, or so that other people would be better off (Brown, Comtois, and Linehan 2002). You might be thinking the same thing—that if you kill yourself, you will feel more at peace, you won't have to deal with your problems anymore, or you might make it so that other people wouldn't have to deal with you or worry about you anymore.

But what if you could solve those problems and not end up dead in the process? Would you still want to be dead? What if there were some way of feeling more peaceful or content more often, feeling more in control of your life, and solving your problems? Would you still want to kill yourself? If you notice that you're thinking about suicide, figure out what it is you really want. Start by taking the following steps:

1. *Think, "Oh, a thought about suicide. This must mean that there's a problem."*
2. *Figure out what the problem is.* The problem could be anything. It could be that something very painful has just happened to you (for example, a partner has broken up with you), and you feel terrible and don't know what to do. Or, it could be that you have felt depressed for a long time and can't see any way out of it. The important thing here is to get yourself thinking about the problem that could be spurring these suicidal thoughts.
3. Figure *out what you want* As we have mentioned, a lot of the time you might just want your problem to go away, or you might want to feel more content or peaceful. So, instead, say to yourself, "I don't

want to be dead, I just want to _____ ." Fill in the blank with your foremost wish, like "feel more peace," "feel better," "escape my emotions," "stop thinking about my problems," or "find a way to make things better."

4. *The next step is to figure out what you can do to get what you want without killing yourself.* If you can't come up with something on your own, then use some of the skills in this book (see chapter 12), look around for other coping skills that might help, call a friend or someone who can give you good advice, or talk with your therapist, if you have one.

5. *Remember that killing yourself is a permanent solution to a temporary problem.* Life surprises us all. What if the solution to your problem is just around the next corner and you never get there because you killed yourself?

When we see people who are having suicidal thoughts, often the first thing we ask them is "Do you want to be dead, or do you want to escape the pain that you're in right now?" Every person we have posed this question to has said, "I want out of the pain." Nobody has said, "I want to be dead." Our clients tell us that they don't think about suicide because their goal is to be dead. Instead, they simply can't come up with another way to feel better or solve their problems. In this way, people sometimes see suicide as the solution, rather than the problem. But remember, there are many other solutions, many other ways to get out of the pain. You just have to find them. And for that, you may need some help—from a therapist, a friend, a family member, a case manager, or perhaps a self-help book such as this one.

## Change the Situation

You would be amazed at what a difference simply getting out of the environment you are in and into a different place can make. If you are at home thinking about suicide, leave and go out somewhere, preferably somewhere with other people around (a restaurant, coffee shop, mall, library, university, and so on). But here's the important thing: don't spend time thinking about going somewhere—just do it. As soon as you think you need to leave your place (or wherever you are), just pick a safe place and get out now while you still can—before you convince yourself not to! When you get where you're going, pay attention to what's going on around you, instead of being stuck in your head the whole time. So pay attention to all of the sights, sounds, smells, and tastes of everything around you. This will allow you to experience the world from a different perspective.

Below is a list of some of the places you might consider going when you are feeling suicidal and need to change your environment right away.

### Table 11.1 Places to Go If You Are Feeling Suicidal and Need to Get Out

- A mall
- A coffee shop
- A restaurant

- A busy park (during the daytime)
- The beach
- The library
- A community center
- A fitness center
- A university's student union building
- The zoo
- A friend's home
- A neighbor's home
- A family member's home

## Think About Reasons to Stay Alive

Another skill that can help you when you are having suicidal thoughts is to think about important reasons not to kill yourself. Back in the 1980s, Dr. Marsha Linehan and her colleagues (1983) came up with a questionnaire called the Reasons for Living Inventory. This questionnaire includes several important reasons that some people have for not killing themselves. Based on Dr. Linehan's work, and from talking to our clients, we have included table 11.2, which lists different types of reasons that sometimes help people not kill themselves.

### Table 11.2 Reasons for Living/Reasons Not to Commit Suicide Reasons Not to Commit Suicide

- Beliefs that you will ultimately be able to make your life better and solve your problems in other ways
- Concerns that you could hurt your family by killing yourself
- Concerns that you would hurt your children, partner, friends, pets, or others whom you care about if you killed yourself
- Fears of dying
- Fears of failing in your suicide attempt and being worse off as a result (being paralyzed, damaging your body, and having medical problems like chronic pain, for example)
- Fears of pain
- Moral or religious objections to suicide

> - Fears of disapproval from other people
> - Fears of something terrible happening to you (like going to hell) if you were to kill yourself

It can be very helpful to think about your reasons for not killing yourself. Look through this list and see if any of these reasons are important to you. Then, come up with your own list of reasons. For instance, think about how killing yourself will affect the people you care about, or think about how killing yourself might make it hard for your children, family, or pet. Imagine the look on your child's face, or the face of your parents, partner, or someone else close to you, if that person found out that you killed yourself. Think about why it makes sense to have hope for the future and encourage yourself: tell yourself that you can get through this, and that you will make things change. Pay attention to the reasons for living that are important to you, and really connect with your reasons for staying alive. Often, we have found that, even in the middle of the most stormy crisis, just a thought about a child or a pet, or just a glimmer of hope, is enough to help stop someone from attempting suicide.

## *Take Action and Challenge Hopeless Thinking*

Time and time again, research studies have shown that hopeless thoughts about the future predict suicidal thinking and behavior (Brown et al. 2000). Suicidal people tend to think more hopeless thoughts about their lives than people who are not suicidal. More specifically, suicidal people seem to be less likely to think that something positive will happen in the future than nonsuicidal people are. They are also less able to come up with reasons why negative events will not happen in the future (MacLeod and Tarbuck 1994).

When you are mired in strong, negative emotions, it can be incredibly difficult to think clearly, and hopeless thinking might dominate your mind. Now, at those times, it is probably not going to be easy for you to think hopeful thoughts. You might find that you tend to "poison" any hopeful thoughts you come up with, saying, for example, "I don't believe that. Nothing is ever going to change." So, we suggest that when you are in the middle of an emotional crisis, the best way to deal with hopeless thinking is to take action right now and avoid *acting* hopeless.

When you are thinking hopeless thoughts, the best actions to take are the ones that tell you that things can actually change. One skill you can use involves "acting opposite" to hopeless thinking. In Dr. Marsha Linehan's dialectical behavior therapy (DBT), one of the important skills used to help people manage their emotions is called "opposite action." This involves acting in a manner that is the opposite of what you feel like doing. So, if you are angry and feel like yelling at someone, the opposite action would be to be kind to the person. If you are afraid and feel like escaping the situation, the opposite action would be to stay in the situation (Linehan 1993b). This might remind some of you of the *Seinfeld* episode where George Costanza decided to do the opposite of everything he normally did. It's not exactly the same thing, of course (and you won't turn into a short, stocky bald man if you do this!), but this strategy can be very useful for dealing with hopeless thoughts. If you are thinking that things are hopeless, then act opposite to these hopeless thoughts. Think about what you would do if you felt very hopeful that things could get better. Then, take action immediately to make things better. You may not be able to solve your life problems right now, but you can probably do something to make yourself feel better, take a small step to solve your problem, or work on accepting what is happening in your life. So, when you have hopeless thoughts, go through the skills we describe in chapter 12, choose one, and take action. Call a friend, talk to your therapist—do anything you can do to get an idea of the first step to take. Taking even the *smallest* step toward making things better can improve your outlook and give you hope that things can change.

But here's an important caveat: this only works if you really pay attention to what happens. Don't take a small step but spend the whole time stuck in your head thinking about how terrible or hopeless things are, or how much you'd like to kill yourself. Keep your eyes and your mind open to what is happening around you right now, and pay attention to the small but important steps that you are making.

## *Let the Thoughts Come and Go*

Another skill that can be very helpful involves simply letting your suicidal thoughts come and go. The fact that you're having thoughts about suicide does not mean that you have to act on these thoughts. They are just thoughts—the activity of your mind. We all have thoughts that we would never act on. You might feel angry with your boss and think about yelling at her or him or throwing things, but (we hope!) you don't act on these thoughts. We might have had the thought that we'd rather be eating pizza or sitting on the beach than writing this book, but if we had acted on those thoughts, you wouldn't be reading this right now!

Thoughts are just thoughts. Sometimes, they are very convincing. They sound and feel true, and it may seem like killing yourself is the thing to do. But you have the freedom to simply let your thoughts come and go, and you do not have to act on them. Below is one exercise that you can use to practice this strategy (similar to some of the exercises in Dr. Steven Hayes's work on acceptance and commitment therapy; Hayes, Strosahl, and Wilson 1999):

> Imagine that you are lying in a large green field and looking up at the sky. It's a peaceful day, warm and sunny, with a slight breeze. In the sky, you see some large, billowing white clouds floating by. Imagine that your thoughts are written on each cloud, and watch the clouds as they float by. Just let them go. Don't follow any one cloud (or thought). Just let them go.

## Use Any of the Emotional Coping Skills Provided in the Next Chapter

As we have mentioned, many people with BPD attempt suicide because they are hoping to escape their intense emotional pain or the misery of their lives. Remember, though, that we don't know whether suicide actually works to help people escape their emotions. For all we know, people who commit suicide are doomed to feel the same thing from now to eternity. And, in order to have the life that you want, you actually have to stay alive! So, if you're looking for a way to feel better, then we suggest that you use skills that work. We talk about some of these skills in the next chapter.

## Summary

*When Alice realized that she was seriously thinking about suicide, she stopped and thought, "Wait a second. What do I really want here? Do I want to die, or do I want to feel less scared, overwhelmed, and lonely?" As it turned out, she really wanted to feel less scared, overwhelmed, and lonely, but she was having a hard time figuring out how she would go about doing this. She was thinking of taking all of her medications at once, so she realized that the best thing to do would be to either get rid of her medications or leave her apartment (or both). So she left her apartment and went to a nearby coffee house, ordered her favorite chocolate croissant, and sat and watched the rain drip down the windows. She felt a little less lonely listening to the buzz of conversation around her, but it just wasn't quite enough. Alice called her friend Molly and told her that she was having a hard time, and Molly soon showed up at the cafe. Alice talked through what was happening, and Molly listened supportively and offered some suggestions about what she could do. Afterward, Alice still felt stressed about her job situation and sad about her breakup, but she wasn't thinking about suicide anymore, and she felt a glimmer of hope that things could get better.*

In this chapter, we have focused on skills that can help you stay alive when you are thinking about suicide. This is critically important, because none of the rest of the skills we discuss in the next chapter will work if you're not alive. Below is a summary of the skills we offered in this chapter. When you're thinking about suicide, do the following things:

- Stay away from things that you could use to kill yourself.
- Change your current situation by going somewhere else where it would be hard to attempt suicide.
- Remind yourself that suicidal thoughts mean that there is a problem. Ask yourself what the problem is and how you might solve it. Figure out what you really want (for example, to escape from your emotions) and begin to work toward getting it.
- Get help from other people.
- Think about reasons to stay alive.

- Take action, challenge hopeless thoughts, and act in a way that is hopeful.
- Let the suicidal thoughts come and go. Watch them as if they are clouds in the sky.
- Use coping strategies to manage your emotions and help yourself feel better. (See chapter 12 for more detailed coping strategies.)

# 12

# Coping with Your Emotions

*John was getting sick of his intense emotions. Even the smallest thing (like a look from someone or a slightly harsh tone of voice) would throw him into a tailspin. He was so emotional that he felt different from everyone else around him. He didn't have any idea of what to do when he was upset. He knew he needed to find some way to cope with his emotions more effectively.*

In this chapter, we discuss some helpful skills you can use to manage your emotions and get yourself through difficult times. If you think you have BPD, or if someone has told you that you have BPD, try following our recommendations in chapter 7 for finding professional help. Then, use the skills in this chapter to help yourself cope as you try to find the right treatment for you, as you are waiting for your treatment to begin, or to help yourself cope with your emotions even when you are in therapy. Of course, although you can help yourself, there is no evidence that self-help alone is enough to treat BPD.

## Skills You Can Use to Cope with Emotions

As you have probably gathered by now, many of the problems that people with BPD face have to do with emotions. Being a very emotional person is not the problem, though. The problem is the way in which some people with BPD cope with their emotions. If you have BPD, you might find yourself doing things impulsively (like doing drugs), harming yourself, or avoiding your emotions at all costs when you feel upset. But, as we've mentioned before, although doing these things might work in the short term, they tend to cause pretty big problems in the long term. Harming yourself might make you feel better for a while, but it can also erode your self-respect, lead to permanent scars, and keep you hooked on hurting yourself as a way to cope with life. Avoiding your emotions might also work in the short term, but in the long term, you will probably end up feeling even worse if you always avoid your emotions. And, avoidance stops you from solving the problems that led to your emotions in the first place! This chapter is the place where you will learn ways to manage emotions more effectively.

The idea behind this chapter is that other, more helpful ways of managing your emotions do not have such unfortunate side effects. Many of the skills we discuss below come directly from Dr. Marsha Linehan's work on dialectical behavior therapy. If you believe these skills may be helpful, you might also be interested in checking out Dr. Linehan's *Skills Training Manual for Treating Borderline Personality Disorder* (1993b).

## *Practice Accepting Your Emotions and Your Situation Right Now*

*Mary slipped and fell at work one day and cracked a disk in her spine. Ever since her injury, Mary has struggled with chronic pain, which often lasts for several hours at a time without letting up. She has undergone two surgeries on her back, but they haven't made any difference in her pain or ability to move around. Even pain medications don't seem to work for very long, and they only dull the pain and leave her in a foggy, lethargic state. She has stopped engaging in the physical activities that she used to enjoy, such as golf and tennis. If she sits for a long period, she has extreme difficulty getting up. Mary also has a young toddler, Sam, and she is no longer able to carry him. After the second surgery failed, she felt desperate, hopeless, and frustrated, and she told her therapist, "I can't stand this! I can't believe this is happening to me. I can't stand feeling so desperate and angry and afraid all the time. I want to die."*

One of the simplest (but hardest) ways to deal with emotions is to practice accepting the feelings you are experiencing, accepting the difficult situation that you are in, or accepting the upsetting things that have happened to you. We say "practice" because accepting your emotions (or anything else for that matter) is really something that you work toward, rather than something that you actually achieve. Accepting is not like passing a final exam and being done with a course; it's more like cleaning your house. You are never quite done with accepting, and you often have to keep doing it again and again. Unlike cleaning your house, however, you can't get someone else to accept your emotions for you.

So, what exactly does accepting your emotions involve? It means simply letting them be exactly as they are. Accepting is the process of stopping the struggle to change, avoid, escape, suppress, or get rid of your emotions.

Instead, you simply let your emotions be there because they are there, and, really, what other choice do you have? If something happens and you feel bad, then you feel bad. Struggling to get rid of that feeling or trying to escape it in some way is often what leads to so many problems, or causes people to do things that create more suffering. So, if you practice accepting your emotions because they are there already, your emotions will actually stop being so much of a problem for you. Just as we talked about with hopeless thoughts in the last chapter, you can simply let your emotions come and go, and know that you don't have to act on them in any particular way. In his book on acceptance and commitment therapy, Dr. Steven Hayes says that struggling with your emotions is like being in a tug-of-war with a huge, strong monster (Hayes, Strosahl, and Wilson 1999). Accepting is dropping the rope and just allowing the monster to be what it is.

Imagine that you live in a very rainy place and you really hate the rain, but it just keeps raining. The more it rains, the more you hate it. In fact, you hate it so much that you refuse to acknowledge that it's even raining at all. So, you go out without a jacket, leave your sunroof open, and ignore everyone who talks about how wet the weather has been. After a while, people start to avoid you because you get weird every time they bring up the weather, and your clothes are always soaked. Whenever you drop your guard and notice that it's raining, you get even more upset. You think about how terrible it is that it's still raining, you lament your decision to live in a rainy place, and you panic every time you watch the weather on the news.

If you have BPD, you might do something similar with your emotions. In fact, many of us do this from time to time even if we don't have BPD. To accept the rain, on the other hand, would be to look out the window and say, "Yes, it's raining. I may not like it, but it is raining, and the weather is what it is." As it turns out, you can do the same thing with your emotions. "Accepting" doesn't mean "liking." You don't have to like your emotions, but if you work on accepting them when they are around you might find that you feel a little more at peace with yourself. You might also find that you are more capable of doing what you need to do in order to reduce your suffering (like putting on a raincoat).

Here's the crucial thing to remember: accepting is not surrendering, giving up, or resigning yourself to emotional suffering and a life that is hopeless (Linehan 1993b). Accepting is not throwing away your life raft and drowning in the ocean of despair. Accepting is simply not fighting things that have happened in the past (in other words, things that you cannot change) or things that are happening *right now,* in the present.

Once you have accepted the thing that is bothering you, you can work to change it (Linehan 1993b). For example, you can accept that you have been fired from your job, but then you can work on getting another job. You can accept that you feel anxious about giving a speech in front of people, but you can find ways to feel a little less anxious. Or, you can accept that you have health problems (such as diabetes), but you can work to manage or improve your health.

All this might sound good, but how do you actually do this? Well, there are many ways to practice accepting your feelings and aspects of your life. Below, we list a few ways to do this:
- Watch your emotions as they come and go. Emotions often arrive as physical sensations in your body (for example, anxiety might come as a racing heart, or knots in your stomach). Watch these physical sensations as they come and go. Just watch them, and let go of them. Don't try to change them, and don't judge them (don't label them as "bad" or "terrible," for example).
- Say to yourself that you accept what you feel right now. Say, "I accept that I feel _____ right now."
- Say to yourself that you accept whatever happened to make you upset. For instance, in Alice's case from chapter 11, she might say, "I accept that I lost my job." You might work on accepting that you have lost your partner or a family member, have a serious health problem, have

been abused in the past, or have simply had to deal with annoying daily hassles.
- Practice stating the event that upset you out loud (for example, "I was fired," "My partner split up with me," "I don't have enough money," or "I weigh more than I would like to weigh") whenever you find yourself struggling with your problems.
- Write down how you feel and just look at what you have written.
- Breathe in and say the word "accept" to yourself in your head. Then, breathe out, and say "accept" again. Just breathe your emotion in and out. (This skill of breathing in and out also appears in the "distress tolerance" section of Dr. Linehan's skills training manual [1993b].)

If you would like to read more about the skill of accepting, we recommend Dr. Linehan's skills training manual (1993b) or Dr. Hayes's book *Get Out of Your Mind and Into Your Life: The New Acceptance and Commitment Therapy* (2005).

*Mary's therapist understood her pain and distress and suggested that they work on acceptance. At first, Mary said, "Are you crazy! You try to accept this. I can't do it. I can't accept that things will always be this way." Mary's therapist told her that she didn't have to accept that things would always be this way. She just had to work on accepting the way things were right then, and maybe pay attention to those times when she is not suffering quite as much (when her back doesn't hurt quite so much). Her therapist also suggested that she work on accepting her emotional reactions (anger, sadness, frustration), since they were perfectly normal reactions to an incredibly stressful situation. Over time, Mary found it easier to accept that she had this injury, and, when she felt sad, frustrated, or angry, she no longer tried to get rid of these emotions and just let them be. She still holds out hope that people will come up with a way to fix her back, but for now she has learned to live with it and to enjoy the times when she is not in pain.*

## *Distraction*

Sometimes, the best way to deal with your emotions when you are really upset is to focus your attention on something else. Distraction is finding something else to pay attention to that gets your mind off of whatever is troubling you. You can distract yourself in many different ways. Below, we list several things that you can do to distract yourself. Again, many of these suggestions come directly from Dr. Linehan's work on DBT (Linehan 1993b).

- *Think about something else* (Linehan 1993b). Count backward from 100 to 0. Start at 115, and keep subtracting 7 until you get to 3. Count the holes in the ceiling tiles. Count the number of floorboards in the room. Count the number of clicks made by the second hand on a clock. Try to come up with the name of an animal or a city that starts with each letter of the alphabet.
- *Do something that gets your mind busy.* Do a crossword puzzle, or another type of activity that gets your brain involved in something

(such as a Sudoku puzzle, math problems, word games, video games, or computer games).
- *Do some work.* Find some work you have to get done and throw yourself into it completely (for example, cleaning your house, washing the dishes, buying groceries, helping someone with something, doing yard work, doing your laundry). When you are doing this chore, make sure you focus as much of your attention on it as possible. Pay attention to just that chore and nothing else. Immerse yourself in it.
- *Do something you enjoy that keeps you busy.* For example, you could do an art or craft project (even if you are not artsy or crafty!). You don't have to paint a picture worthy of Monet. It can be as simple as coloring in a coloring book, sketching an image, or doing a collage. If you are into martial arts or some other kind of physical activity, go ahead and do it. Go out for a walk through a pleasant area, go to your favorite restaurant or coffee shop, or spend time with someone whom you really

enjoy (you could even do this via phone, instant messaging, or e-mail).
- *Use your imagination* (Linehan 1993b). Imagine that you are in your favorite vacation spot (perhaps a beach on a Caribbean island). Put yourself into your favorite fantasy, and really get into it (provided that it doesn't involve harming yourself). Imagine that you are successfully dealing with your problems. Imagine that you are in a very peaceful place, such as sitting in a grassy field by a gently flowing stream on a warm day. Imagine all of the sights, sounds, smells, tastes, and touch sensations that you might experience in the situation you are imagining.
- *Listen to music that will pull you out of your current emotion.* For example, listen to loud and energizing music if you are sad or feeling down, or listen to soft, soothing music if you are feeling anxious, tense, or angry. This operates on the same principle as the DBT distraction skill in which you do something that triggers "opposite

emotions" (Linehan 1993b). The next item also follows this principle.

- *Watch a television show or movie that grabs your attention.* Choose something with a mood that's opposite of what you are feeling. For example, if you are feeling sadness or some other emotion that makes you feel low in energy or motivation, watch a show or movie that is exciting (like a suspense movie) or funny. On the other hand, if you are feeling angry, agitated, tense, or stressed, watch something that might be more soothing.
- *Go out and do something.* Get active and do things that grab your attention. Call up one of your friends and go out to do something that gets your mind off your problems for a little while.
- *Do something to stimulate one (or all) of your five senses* (Linehan 1993b). If you want to distract yourself from a very intense emotion, it can be helpful to introduce something intense or different into your environment. It just might capture your attention and jolt you

into contact with that sensation and out of contact with your emotions. This skill can be applied using each of the five senses. These skills (activating the five senses, listed below) come directly from the "self-soothing" skills in Linehan's skills training manual (1993b). See her manual for an expanded discussion of these skills.

- *Taste:* Keep strong-flavored candies with you to suck on when you feel upset. Good choices are strong cinnamon candies, sour lemon drops, and strongly flavored mints. Another option that some people find helpful is to eat salt-and-vinegar potato chips; place a chip on the edge of your tongue and just leave it there for a while.
- *Touch:* Focus on things that have a distinct texture or temperature. Run cold or very warm water over your hands. Hold a piece of ice in your hand until it melts. Stand under a very hard, hot shower (but not so hot that it burns). Grab your chair and hold it as tightly as you can; feel the

tension building in your hands and arms. Touch various objects around you, such as keys, a zipper, or upholstery. Notice how the textures feel against your fingers. Dig your heels into the floor and notice what sensations you feel. Notice the tension in your legs and the pressure against the soles of your feet.

- *Smell:* Look for smells that are really strong. Slice an onion and breathe in the fumes. Go to your spice rack and start smelling the different spices. Spray perfume or cologne on a piece of paper and smell it. Burn incense. Brew a fresh pot of coffee and smell the aroma.
- *Hearing:* Listen to loud music. Blow a horn or buzzer several times. Blow on a whistle.
- *Sight:* Focus on an image that really captures your attention. This could be something beautiful in nature (a gorgeous sunset, or a beautiful flower). Or it could also be a picture of a loved one, a favorite painting, or an inspirational poem or saying that really speaks

to you. Focus your attention on every aspect of the image.

Keep in mind that it's possible to overuse distraction. You might find that these techniques work so well that you're always distracting yourself whenever you get upset. Depending on what you use to distract yourself, this might not be as harmful as hurting yourself, using drugs, or attempting suicide. But constantly distracting yourself can turn into avoidance, and by now you probably remember that too much avoidance can increase your suffering and can stop you from solving or accepting your problems. So, we suggest that you use this skill in moderation, in order to make it through a difficult time. Then, when the storm or crisis has passed, stop distracting yourself and face your problems and your emotions.

## *Relaxation Strategies*

Most treatments for anxiety disorders involve skills to help people relax, and many people find these skills to be quite helpful. But, these skills are helpful not only for managing anxiety but for managing other emotions as well, such as anger. These skills tend to work best for emotions that get you all charged up or feeling tense, agitated, or energized. The two most common relaxation skills are *progressive muscle relaxation* and *diaphragmatic breathing*. Simply slowing down your breathing can also be helpful.

Before we go into what these skills are, we want to make sure you know one very important thing: it is very important that you don't spend the whole time worrying while you're practicing these skills. If you are anxious or stressed, you might have the tendency to worry about the future. This will make you even more anxious. So, when you are practicing these skills, do your best to keep your attention focused on the present and on what your body feels like in the moment. And, if you feel your mind starting to wander off or if you start to worry about the future, just bring your attention back to the exercise you are doing.

## Progressive Muscle Relaxation

Progressive muscle relaxation, or PMR for short, is a way of reducing tension and anxiety, and, sometimes, anger. In order to do this, find a quiet place where you won't be disturbed, and get into a comfortable position. You can do this lying down, sitting up, or even standing up, but you may find that it works best if you are lying down.

PMR basically involves tensing and relaxing different muscles of your body. The idea behind this skill is that it is easier to relax your muscles if you do so after you purposefully tense them. If you try to relax your muscles as you go about your day, with your normal amount of tension, you might not be able to relax them as much as you will if you tighten them up a lot and then try to relax them from there. Think of this as like pushing a child on a swing. If you lift the swing up high when you're starting, it will swing forward much higher than it would if you were to lift it up just a little before releasing it.

1. The first thing to do is find a place to start. There is really no "right"

place to begin. You might decide to start with the top of your head or the tips of your toes. Let's say that you are starting with your toes.
2. Bring your full attention to your toes. Imagine that your whole brain is being drawn down to the tips of your toes. Then, curl your toes inward toward the bottoms of your feet until you feel tension in your toes. Tense your toes to about 75 to 80 percent of your maximum strength, and hold them tense for about five to ten seconds.
3. Then, let your toes go, and relax your muscles. Notice the difference between how they felt when they were tense and how they feel now. Just notice any relaxation, warmth, or any other sensations you might experience.
4. Now, move up to your ankles. Create tension in your ankles by tensing your feet. Hold it for five to ten seconds again, then let it go, and relax your feet and ankles. Notice the difference between the

feeling of tension and the feeling of relaxation.

5. Keep going all the way up your body to the top of your head, doing exactly the same thing. Each time, just tense your muscles about 75 to 80 percent (or more, if it does not hurt to do so) for about five to ten seconds, and then relax them, and notice the difference. Do PMR for anywhere from five minutes to twenty-five minutes, depending on how much time you have. Even doing it for five minutes can make a difference.

There are two main goals for this skill: (1) to help you notice the difference between the feeling of having tense muscles and having relaxed muscles, and (2) to help you feel more relaxed. People often say that they feel at least 50 percent more relaxed after they do this exercise.

This is a good skill to use when you feel tense, anxious, agitated, overwhelmed, stressed, or angry, and it can work very well for some people. One of us was seeing a client who said that he knew of no way to get his anxiety down, and he was feeling quite anxious during the therapy session (85 on a scale of 0 to 100, where 100 means the highest possible anxiety). After only ten minutes of doing PMR, his anxiety was down to 40 out of 100, and he continues to use this skill when he wants to get his anxiety down.

**Diaphragmatic Breathing**

Diaphragmatic breathing is another skill that can be helpful for emotions such as anxiety, anger, agitation, and feelings of tension or being stressed out. This skill is really simple. It simply involves breathing slowly and deliberately through your diaphragm. Breathing through your diaphragm provides you with the fullest, deepest breaths possible, which is really important when you are trying to calm down and relax.

Just like with PMR, it can be helpful to start practicing this skill in a quiet place where people won't interrupt you. First, sit in an upright position and put one hand on your chest and one hand on your abdomen. Then, breathe in whatever way you normally breathe. Notice which hand seems to be moving more—your hand on your chest or your hand on your abdomen. Many people notice that the hand on their chest moves more, which indicates that they are not breathing with their diaphragm.

As you continue breathing, make sure that you are drawing the air into your lungs mainly through your abdomen. Work at this until you notice that your lower hand is moving more than your upper hand. Then, slow down your breathing, so it's a little slower than you normally breathe, but not so slow that you feel as if you aren't getting enough air. Also, deepen your breathing, so that you're breathing deeper than normal, but not so deep that you feel like a big balloon that is about to explode. Just sit, and breathe in and out through your abdomen slowly and deliberately. You can also imagine that as you breathe, the tension is draining out of your body, or coming out of your mouth like a mist or steam.

This skill can help for a couple of reasons. First, it's common to breathe through your chest when you are anxious or tense. Unfortunately, breathing through your chest actually can make you feel more anxious or tense, especially if you tend to hyperventilate. Breathing through your abdomen or diaphragm actually brings more air deeper into your lungs, so you get a better exchange of oxygen and carbon dioxide. Second, breathing can help you slow down and can give you something to focus your attention on. When something has just happened and you're really upset, giving yourself time to just breathe for a little while can help calm your mind and give you space to think about what to do. Of course, as we mentioned above, save the thinking until after you're done with the breathing exercise. When you're breathing (or doing PMR), just breathe. Leave the thinking, planning, and problem solving for later, when you feel a little calmer.

Now, one thing to keep in mind with both of these relaxation skills is that once you have practiced them a little and know what to expect, you can use them in your daily life when something happens to stress you out. The way we are presenting them here can be considered a more formal relaxation practice, which you can use every day, or when you are stressed, or tense, or irritable. Take some time to really focus on relaxing your body and calming your mind. In fact, many people find that doing PMR or diaphragmatic breathing in this more formal way can be a good way to destress or relax at the end of a long day. It can also help you sleep better at night if you have problems sleeping. However, this is just one way to use these skills.

Another way to practice them is to use them informally, in the moment, when something happens to stress you out or upset you. If you find yourself feeling really upset, agitated, or anxious, you can do a mini-PMR exercise or a bit of diaphragmatic breathing to calm down before responding. You don't need a quiet space, a place to sit or lie down, or a lot of time. Instead, use these skills informally anytime and anywhere, just to take the edge off your frustration or anxiety. You can also use the next skill (slowing down your breathing) in this informal way to help yourself calm down at any time when you notice that you are starting to feel really anxious.

**Slowing Down Your Breathing**

The final skill related to relaxation is to simply slow down your breathing. As we mentioned before, many people take shallow, quick breaths when they are anxious or upset. But, this can actually make you feel more anxious! So, one way to help you calm down a bit when you notice you are doing this is to focus all of your attention on slowing down your breathing. It can be as simple as counting to six as you breathe out. So, take a deep breath and then slowly count to six as you breathe out. Then, take another deep breath and do this again, over and over. Or, if you find that counting to six doesn't make your exhale as long as it could be to really slow down your breathing, you can start by counting to six, and then count to eight the next time, and then ten the next time, until your breathing is really slow. Not only will this skill help you slow down your breathing, but it also gives you something to focus your attention on (that is, counting), which can help distract you from your troubles for the moment.

## Summary

*After learning some skills to cope with her emotions, Mary came up with a plan that she would put into action whenever she felt emotionally overwhelmed. First, she would slow down her breathing and just pay attention to what was happening right then. Next, she would practice accepting whatever had happened and whatever she was feeling. If this was too much of a struggle, she would find some way to distract herself. Crossword puzzles or listening to music really worked for Mary. Then, once she felt less overwhelmed, she would figure out what to do to change things for herself.*

In this chapter, we have focused on coping skills that can help you to manage your emotions. As we have mentioned, BPD is an emotional disorder. If you have BPD, you probably struggle with your emotions at times. Maybe you have strong emotions that you wish you didn't have, or maybe you can't tolerate your emotions, try to avoid them, or do act in ways that harm yourself in order to get rid of them. One of the most important steps in recovering from BPD involves learning how to manage your emotions. Below is a summary of some of the skills that we have discussed in this chapter that can help you do just that.

- Practice accepting your emotions, or the difficulties in life that you are struggling with.
- Distract yourself by getting your attention focused on something else.
- Choose distracting activities that help you get your mind busy, or that activate your senses.
- Use progressive muscle relaxation (PMR) to help yourself relax, especially if you feel anxious, afraid, tense, agitated, or angry.

- Use diaphragmatic breathing or slow down your breathing to help yourself relax.
- Practice these skills as often as you can, so that you will be really comfortable with using them when you really need them.

# References

Ainsworth, M.D., S.M. Bell, and D.J. Stayton. 1971. Individual differences in strange situation behaviour of one-year-olds. In *The Origins of Human Social Relations,* edited by H.R. Shaeffer. London: Academic Press.

American Psychiatric Association. 2000. *Diagnostic and Statistical Manual of Mental Disorders (DSM-IV-TR).* 4th ed. Text revision. Washington, DC: American Psychiatric Association.

Axelrod, S.R., A. Morgan III, and S.M. Southwick. 2005. Symptoms of posttraumatic stress disorder and borderline personality disorder in veterans of Operation Desert Storm. *American Journal of Psychiatry* 162:270–75.

Baer, J., and C.D. Martinez. 2006. Child maltreatment and insecure attachment: A meta-analysis. *Journal of Reproductive and Infant Psychology* 24:187–91.

Ball, S.A., H. Tennen, J.C. Poling, H.R. Kranzler, and B.J. Rounsaville. 1997. Personality, temperament, and character dimensions and the *DSM-IV* personality disorders in substance abusers. *Journal of Abnormal Psychology* 106:545–53.

Baron, M., R. Gruen, and L. Asnis. 1985. Familial transmission of schizotypal borderline personality disorders. *American Journal of Psychiatry* 142:927–34.

Bateman, A.W., and P. Fonagy. 1999. Effectiveness of partial hospitalization in the treatment of borderline personality disorder: A randomized controlled trial. *American Journal of Psychiatry* 156:1563–69.

———. 2001. Treatment of borderline personality disorder with psychoanalytically oriented partial hospitalization: An eighteen-month follow-up. *American Journal of Psychiatry* 158:36–42.

———. 2004. Mentalization-based treatment of BPD. *Journal of Personality Disorders* 18:36–51.

Baumeister, R.F. 1990. Suicide as escape from self. *Psychological Review* 97:90–113.

Behavioral Tech LLC. 2004. *Sitting In on Therapy with Marsha Linehan, Ph.D., ABPP: Assessing and Treating Suicidal Behaviors.* VHS. Seattle, WA: Behavioral Tech LLC.

Benedetti, F., L. Sforzini, C. Colombo, C. Maffei, and E. Smeraldi. 1998. Low-dose clozapine in acute and continuation treatment of severe borderline personality disorder. *Journal of Clinical Psychiatry* 59:103–7.

Bogenschutz, M.P., and H.G. Nurnberg. 2004. Olanzapine versus placebo in the treatment of borderline personality disorder. *Journal of Clinical Psychiatry* 65:104–9.

Brodsky, B.S., K.M. Malone, and S.P. Ellis. 1997. Characteristics of borderline personality disorder associated with suicidal behavior. *American Journal of Psychiatry* 154:1715–19.

Brown, G.K., A.T. Beck, R.A. Steer, and J.R. Grisham. 2000. Risk factors for suicide in psychiatric outpatients: A twenty-year prospective study. *Journal of Consulting and Clinical Psychology* 68:371–77.

Brown, M.Z., and A.L. Chapman. 2007. Stopping self-harm once and for all: Relapse prevention in dialectical behavior therapy. In *Therapist's Guide to Evidence-Based Relapse Prevention,* edited by G.A. Marlatt and K. Witkiewitz. London: Academic Press.

Brown, M.Z., K.A. Comtois, and M.M. Linehan. 2002. Reasons for suicide attempts and nonsuicidal self-injury in women with borderline personality disorder. *Journal of Abnormal Psychology* 111:198–202.

Carrion, V.G., C.F. Weems, R.D. Ray, B. Glaser, D. Hessl, and A.L. Reiss. 2002. Diurnal salivary cortisol in pediatric PTSD. *Biological Psychiatry* 51:575–82.

Chapman, A.L., and K.L. Dixon-Gordon. Forthcoming. Emotional antecedents and consequences of deliberate self-harm and suicide attempts. *Suicide and Life Threatening Behavior.*

Chapman, A.L., K.L. Gratz, and M.Z. Brown. 2006. Solving the puzzle of deliberate self-harm: The experiential avoidance model. *Behaviour Research and Therapy* 44:371–94.

Chapman, A.L., and M.M. Linehan. 2005. Dialectical behavior therapy for borderline personality disorder. In *Borderline Personality Disorder,* edited by M. Zanarini. Boca Raton, FL: Taylor & Francis.

Chengappa, K.N.R., T. Ebeling, J.S. Kang, J. Levine, and H. Parepally. 1999. Clozapine reduces severe self-mutilation and aggression in psychotic patients with borderline personality disorder. *Journal of Clinical Psychiatry* 60:477–84.

Clarkin, J.F., T.A. Widiger, A. Frances, S.W. Hurt, and M. Gilmore. 1983. Prototypic typology and the borderline personality disorder. *Journal of Abnormal Psychology* 92:263–75.

Cornelius, J.R., P.H. Soloff, J.M. Perel, and R.F. Ulrich. 1990. Fluoxetine trial in borderline personality disorder. *Psychopharmacological Bulletin* 26:151–54.

Cowdry, R.W., D. Pickar, and R. Davies. 1985. Symptoms and EEG findings in the borderline syndrome. *International Journal of Psychiatry Medicine* 15:201–11.

Dallman, M.F., N. Pecoraro, S.F. Akana, S.E. la Fleur, F. Gomez, H. Houshyar, M.E. Bell, S. Bhatnagar, K.D. Laugero, and S. Manalo. 2003. Chronic stress and obesity: A new view of "comfort food." *Proceedings of the National Academy of Sciences of the United States of America* 100(20):11696–701.

Damasio, A.R. 1994. *Descartes' Error: Emotion, Reason, and the Human Brain.* New York: G.P. Putnam.

Ebstein, R.P., O. Novick, R. Umansky, B. Priel, Y. Osher, D. Blaine, E.R. Bennett, L. Nemanov, M. Katz, and R.H. Belmaker. 1996. Dopamine D4 receptor (D4DR) exon III polymorphism associated with the human personality trait of Novelty Seeking. *Nature Genetics* 12:78–80.

Essex, M.J., M.H. Klein, E. Cho, and N.H. Kalin. 2002. Maternal stress beginning in infancy may sensitize children to later stress exposure: Effects on cortisol and behavior. *Biological Psychiatry* 52:776–84.

Farmer, R.F., and R.O. Nelson-Gray. 1995. Anxiety, impulsivity, and the anxious fearful and erratic dramatic personality disorders. *Journal of Research in Personality* 29:189.

Frances, A.J., M.R. Fyer, and J.F. Clarkin. 1986. Personality and suicide.

*Annals of the New York Academy of Sciences* 487:281–93.

Frankenburg, F.R., and M.C. Zanarini. 1993. Clozapine treatment in borderline patients: A preliminary study. *Comprehensive Psychiatry* 34:402–5.

———. 2002. Divalproex sodium treatment of women with borderline personality disorder and bipolar II disorder: A double-blind placebo-controlled pilot study. *Journal of Clinical Psychiatry* 63:442–46.

Gladwell, M. 2000. *The Tipping Point: How Little Things Can Make a Big Difference.* Boston: Little, Brown.

Gratz, K.L., D.M. Lacroce, and J.G. Gunderson. 2006. Measuring changes in symptoms relevant to borderline personality disorder following short-term treatment across partial hospital and intensive outpatient levels of care. *Journal of Psychiatric Practice* 12:153–59.

Grilo, C.M., C.A. Sanislow, J.G. Gunderson, M.E. Pagano, S. Yen, M.C. Zanarini, M.T. Shea, et al. 2004. Two-year stability and change of schizotypal, borderline, avoidant, and obsessive-compulsive personality disorders. *Journal of Consulting and Clinical Psychology* 72:767–75.

Grossman, R., R. Yehuda, and L. Siever. 1997. The dexamethasone suppression test and glucocorticoid receptors in borderline personality disorder. In *The Neurobiology of Posttraumatic Stress Disorder,* edited by R. Yehuda and A. McFarlane. New York: New York Academy of Sciences.

Grove, W.M., and A. Tellegen. 1991. Problems in the classification of personality disorders. *Journal of Personality Disorders* 5:31–41.

Gunderson, J.G. 1984. *Borderline Personality Disorder.* Washington, DC: American Psychiatric Press.

———. 1996. The borderline patient's intolerance of aloneness: Insecure attachments and therapist availability. *American Journal of Psychiatry* 153:752–58.

———. 2001. *Borderline Personality Disorder: A Clinical Guide.* Washington, DC: American Psychiatric Publishing.

Gunderson, J.G., D. Bender, C. Sanislow, S. Yen, J.B. Rettew, R. Dolan-Sewell, I. Dyck, et al. 2003. Plausibility and possible determinants of sudden "remissions" in borderline patients. *Psychiatry* 66:111–19.

Gunderson, J.G., K.L. Gratz, E. Neuhaus, and G. Smith. 2005. Levels of care in the treatment of personality disorders. In *Textbook of Personality Disorders,* edited by J.M. Oldham, A.E. Skodol, and D.E. Bender. Washington, DC: American Psychiatric Publishing.

Gunderson, J.G., L.C. Morey, R.L. Stout, A.E. Skodol, M.T. Shea, T.H. McGlashan, M.C. Zanarini, et al. 2004. Major depressive disorder and borderline personality disorder revisited:

Longitudinal interactions. *Journal of Clinical Psychiatry* 65:1049–56.

Gunderson, J.G., M.T. Shea, A.E. Skodol, T.H. McGlashan, L.C. Morey, R.L. Stout, M.C. Zanarini, C.M. Grilo, J.M. Oldham, and M.B. Keller. 2000. The Collaborative Longitudinal Personality Disorders Study: Development, aims, design, and sample characteristics. *Journal of Personality Disorders* 14:300–315.

Haines, J., C. Williams, K. Brain, and G. Wilson. 1995. The psychophysiology of self-mutilation. *Journal of Abnormal Psychology* 104:479–89.

Hanh, T.N. 1976. *The Miracle of Mindfulness: A Manual on Meditation.* Boston: Beacon Press. Hayes, S.C. 2005. *Get Out of Your Mind and Into Your Life: The New Acceptance and Commitment Therapy.* Oakland, CA: New Harbinger Publications.

Hayes, S.C., K.D. Strosahl, and K.G. Wilson. 1999. *Acceptance and Commitment Therapy: An Experiential*

*Approach to Behavior Change.* New York: Guilford Press.

Henry, C., V. Mitropoulou, A.S. New, H.W. Koenigsberg, J. Silverman, and L.J. Siever. 2001. Affective instability and impulsivity in borderline personality and bipolar II disorders: Similarities and differences. *Journal of Psychiatric Research* 35:307–12.

Herman, J.L. 1992. *Trauma and Recovery.* New York: Basic Books.

Herpertz, S.C., T.M. Dietrich, B. Wenning, T. Krings, S.G. Erberich, K. Willmes, A. Thron, and H. Sass. 2001. Evidence of abnormal amygdala functioning in borderline personality disorder: A functional MRI study. *Biological Psychiatry* 50:292–98.

Hollander, E., A. Allen, R.P. Lopez, C. Bienstock, R. Grossman, L. Siever, L. Margolin, and D.A. Stein. 2001. A preliminary doubleblind, placebo-controlled trial of divalproex sodium in borderline personality disorder. *Journal of Clinical Psychiatry* 62:199–203.

Jacobson, N.S., K.S. Dobson, P.A. Truax, M.E. Addis, K. Koerner, J.K. Gollan, E. Gortner, and S.E. Prince. 1996. A component analysis of cognitive-behavioral treatment for depression. *Journal of Consulting and Clinical Psychology* 64:295–304.

Jick, H., J.A. Kaye, and S.S. Jick. 2004. Antidepressants and risk of suicidal behaviors. *Journal of the American Medical Association* 292:338–43.

Johnson, T.D., and L. Edwards. 2002. Genes, interactions, and the development of behavior. *Psychological Review* 109:26–34.

Kaye, W.H., T.E. Weltzin, L.K. Hsu, C.W. McConaha, and B. Bolton. 1993. Amount of calories retained after binge eating and vomiting. *American Journal of Psychiatry* 150:969–71.

Koenigsberg, H.W., P.D. Harvey, V. Mitropoulou, J. Schmeidler, A.S. New,

M. Goodman, J.M. Silverman, M. Serby, F. Schopick, and L.J. Siever. 2002. Characterizing affective instability in borderline personality disorder. *American Journal of Psychiatry* 159:784–88.

Lenzenweger, M.F., M.C. Lane, A.W. Loranger, and R.C. Kessler. Forthcoming. DSM-IV personality disorders in the National Comorbidity Survey Replication. *Biological Psychiatry.*

Lesch, K.P., D. Bengel, A. Heils, S.Z. Sabols, B.D. Greenberg, S. Petri, J. Benjamin, D.H. Hamer, and D.L. Murphy. 1996. Association of anxiety-related traits with a polymorphism in the serotonin transporter gene regulator region. *Science* 274:1527–31.

Lesch, K.P., and A. Heils. 2000. Serotonin gene transcription control regions: Target for antidepressant drug development. *International Journal of Neuropsychopharmacology* 3:67–69.

Lieb, K., J.E. Rexhausen, K.G. Kahl, U. Schweiger, A. Philipsen, D. Hellhammer, M. Bohus, et al. 2004. Increased diurnal salivary cortisol in women with borderline personality disorder. *Journal of Psychiatric Research* 38:559–65.

Lieb, K., M.C. Zanarini, C. Schmahl, M.M. Linehan, and M. Bohus. 2004. Borderline personality disorder. *Lancet* 364:453–61.

Linehan, M.M. 1993a. *Cognitive-Behavioral Treatment of Borderline Personality Disorder.* New York: Guilford Press.

———. 1993b. *Skills Training Manual for Treating Borderline Personality Disorder.* New York: Guilford Press.

Linehan, M.M. 2005. Personal communication. University of Washington, Seattle.

Linehan, M.M., H.E. Armstrong, A. Suarez, D. Allmon, and H. Heard. 1991. Cognitive behavioral treatment of chronically parasuicidal borderline patients. *Archives of General Psychiatry* 48:1060–64.

Linehan, M.M., K.A. Comtois, A.M. Murray, M.Z. Brown, R.J. Gallop, H.L. Heard, K.E. Korslund, D.A. Tutek, S.K. Reynolds, and N. Lindenboim. 2006. Two-year randomized controlled trial and follow-up of dialectical behavior therapy vs. therapy by experts for suicidal behaviors and borderline personality disorder. *Archives of General Psychiatry* 63:757–66.

Linehan, M.M., J.L. Goodstein, S.L. Nielsen, and J.A. Chiles. 1983. Reasons for staying alive when you are thinking of killing yourself: The Reasons for Living Inventory. *Journal of Consulting and Clinical Psychology* 31:276–86.

Linehan, M.M., S.L. Rizvi, S. Shaw-Welch, and B. Page. 2000. Psychiatric aspects of suicidal behaviour: Personality disorders. In *International Handbook of Suicide and Attempted Suicide,* edited by K. Hawton and K. van Heeringen. Hoboken, NJ: John Wiley.

Linehan, M.M., H.I. Schmidt, L.A. Dimeff, J.C. Craft, J. Kanter, and K.A. Comtois. 1999. Dialectical behavior therapy for patients with borderline personality disorder and drug-dependence. *American Journal on Addictions* 8:279–92.

Links, P.S., M. Steiner, I. Boiago, and D. Irwin. 1990. Lithium therapy for borderline patients: Preliminary findings. *Journal of Personality Disorders* 4:173–81.

Links, P.S., M. Steiner, and G. Huxley. 1988. The occurrence of borderline personality disorder in the families of borderline patients. *Journal of Personality Disorders* 2:14–20.

Livesley, W.J., K.L. Jang, and P.A. Vernon. 1998. Phenotypic and genetic structure of traits delineating personality disorder. *Archives of General Psychiatry* 55:941–48.

Lynch, T.R., A.L. Chapman, M.Z. Rosenthal, J.K. Kuo, and M.M. Linehan. 2006. Mechanisms of change in dialectical behavior therapy: Theoretical and empirical observations. *Journal of Clinical Psychology* 62:459-80.

MacLeod, A.K., and A.F. Tarbuck. 1994. Explaining why negative events will happen to oneself: Parasuicides are pessimistic because they can't see any reason not to be. *British Journal of Clinical Psychology* 33:317–26.

Manfo, G.G., M.W. Otto, E.T. McArdle, J.J. Worthington III, J.F. Rosenbaum, and M.H. Pollack. 1996. Relationship of antecedent stressful life events to childhood and family history of anxiety and the course of panic disorder. *Journal of Affective Disorders* 41:135–39.

Markovitz, P.J. 1995. Pharmacotherapy of impulsivity, aggression, and related disorders. In *Impulsivity and Aggression,* edited by E. Hollander and D. Stein. West Sussex, England: John Wiley.

Markovitz, P.J., S.C. Calabrese, and H.Y. Meltzer. 1991. Fluoxetine in the treatment of borderline and schizotypal personality disorders. *American Journal of Psychiatry* 148:1064–67.

Markovitz, P.J., and S.C. Wagner. 1995. Venlafaxine in the treatment of borderline personality disorder. *Psychopharmacological Bulletin* 31:773–77.

Morey, L.C., J.G. Gunderson, B.D. Quigley, M.T. Shea, A.E. Skodol, T.H. McGlashan, R.L. Stout, et al. 2002. The representation of borderline, avoidant, obsessive-compulsive, and schizotypal personality disorders by the five-factor model. *Journal of Personality Disorders* 16:215–34.

Muraven, M., D.M. Tice, and R.F. Baumeister. 1998. Self-control as a limited resource: Regulatory depletion patterns. *Journal of Personality and Social Psychology* 74:774–89.

Norden, M.J. 1989. Fluoxetine in borderline personality disorder. *Progressive*

*Neuro-Psychopharmacological Biological Psychiatry* 13:885–93.

Paris, J. 2005. Recent advancements in the treatment of borderline personality disorder. *Canadian Journal of Psychiatry* 50:435–41.

Parker, G., K. Roy, K. Wilhelm, P. Mitchell, M.P. Austin, and D. Hadzi-Pavlovic. 1999. An exploration of links between early parenting experiences and personality disorder type and disordered personality functioning. *Journal of Personality Disorders* 13:361–74.

Rinne, T., W. van den Brink, L. Wouters, and R. van Dyck. 2002. SSRI treatment of borderline personality disorder: A randomized, placebo-controlled clinical trial for female patients with borderline personality disorder. *American Journal of Psychiatry* 159:2048–54.

Robins, C.J., and A.L. Chapman. 2004. Dialectical behavior therapy: Current status, recent developments, and future directions. *Journal of Personality Disorders* 18:73–79.

Rocca, P., L. Marchiaro, E. Cocuzza, and F. Bogetto. 2002. Treatment of borderline personality disorder with risperidone. *Journal of Clinical Psychiatry* 63:241–44.

Safer, D.L., C.F. Telch, and W.S. Agras. 2001. Dialectical behavior therapy for bulimia nervosa. *American Journal of Psychiatry* 158:632–34.

Salzman, C., A.N. Wolfson, A. Schatzberg, J. Looper, R. Henke, M. Albanese, J. Schwartz, and E. Miyawaki. 1995. Effect of fluoxetine on anger in symptomatic volunteers with borderline personality disorder. *Journal of Clinical Psychopharmacology* 15:23–29.

Schalling, D. 1978. Psychopathy-related personality variables and the psychophysiology of socialization. In *Psychopathic Behavior: Approaches to Research,* edited by R.D. Hare and D. Schalling. New York: John Wiley.

Schmahl, C.G., B.M. Elzinga, E. Vermetten, C. Sanislow, T.H. McGlashan, and J.D. Bremner. 2003. Neural correlates of memories of abandonment in women with and without borderline personality disorder. *Biological Psychiatry* 54:142–51.

Schulz, S.C., K.L. Camlin, S. Berry, and L. Friedman. 1999. Risperidone for borderline personality disorder: A double-blind study. Paper presented at the annual meeting of the American College of Neuropsychopharmacology, Nashville, TN.

Silk, K.R., S. Lee, E.M. Hill, and N.E. Lohr. 1995. Borderline personality disorder and severity of sexual abuse. *American Journal of Psychiatry* 152:1059–64.

Silk, K.R., T.L. Wolf, and D.A. Ben-Ami. 2005. Environmental factors in the etiology of borderline personality disorder. In *Borderline Personality Disorder,* edited by M. Zanarini. Boca Raton, FL: Taylor & Francis.

Skodol, A.E., J.G. Gunderson, B. Pfohl, T.A. Widiger, W.J. Livesley, and L.J. Siever. 2002. The borderline diagnosis I: Psychopathology, comorbidity, and personality structure. *Biological Psychiatry* 51:936.

Skodol, A.E., J.G. Gunderson, M.T. Shea, T.H. McGlashan, L.C. Morey, C.A. Sanislow, D.S. Bender, et al. 2005. The Collaborative Longitudinal Personality Disorders Study (CLPS): Overview and implications. *Journal of Personality Disorders* 19:487–504.

Stein, D.J., D. Simeon, M. Frenkel, M.N. Islam, and E. Hollander. 1995. An open trial of valproate in borderline personality disorder. *Journal of Clinical Psychiatry* 56:506–10.

Stiglmayr, C.E., T. Grathwol, M.M. Linehan, G. Ihorst, J. Fahrenberg, and M. Bohus. 2005. Aversive tension in patients with borderline personality disorder: A computer-based controlled field study. *Acta Psychiatrica Scandinavica* 111:372–79.

Stone, M.H. 1993. Long-term outcome in personality disorders. *British Journal of Psychiatry* 162:299–313.

———. 2005. Borderline personality disorder: History of the concept. In *Borderline Personality Disorder,* edited by M. Zanarini. Boca Raton, FL: Taylor & Francis.

Strobel, A., M. Frank, F.M. Spinath, A. Angleitner, R. Riemann, and K.P. Lesch. 2003. Lack of association between polymorphisms of the dopamine D4 receptor gene and personality. *Neuropsychobiology* 47:52–56.

Swann, W.B., J.G. Hixon, A. Stein-Seroussi, and D.T. Gilbert. 1990. The fleeting gleam of praise: Cognitive processes underlying behavioral reactions to self-relevant feedback. *Journal of Personality and Social Psychology* 59:17–26.

Tebartz van Elst, L., B. Hesslinger, T. Thiel, E. Geiger, K. Haegele, L. Lemieux, K. Lieb, and M. Bohus. 2003. Frontolimbic brain abnormalities in patients with borderline personality disorder: A volumetric magnetic resonance imaging study. *Biological Psychiatry* 54:163–71.

Telch, C.F., W.S. Agras, and M.M. Linehan. 2001. Dialectical behavior therapy for binge eating disorder. *Journal of Consulting and Clinical Psychology* 69:1061–65.

Tice, D.M., E. Bratslavsky, and R.F. Baumeister. 2001. Emotional distress regulation takes precedence over impulse control: If you feel bad, do it! *Journal of Personality and Social Psychology* 80:53–67.

Torgersen, S. 2005. Genetics of borderline personality disorder. In *Borderline Personality Disorder,* edited by M. Zanarini. Boca Raton, FL: Taylor & Francis.

Torgersen, S., S. Lygren, P.A. Oien, S. Onstad, J. Edvardsen, K. Tambs, and E. Kringlen. 2000. A twin study of personality disorders. *Comprehensive Psychiatry* 41:416–25.

Trull, T.J., K.J. Sher, C. Minks-Brown, J. Durbin, and R. Burr. 2000. Borderline personality disorder and substance use disorders: A review and integration. *Clinical Psychology Review* 20:235–53.

van Heeringen, K., K. Audenaert, L. Van de Wiele, and A. Verstraete. 2000. Cortisol in violent suicidal behaviour: Association with personality and monoaminergic activity. *Journal of Affective Disorders* 60:181–89.

Welch, S.S., and M.M. Linehan. 2002. High-risk situations associated with parasuicide and drug use in borderline personality disorder. *Journal of Personality Disorders* 16:561–69.

Whittington, C., R. Kendall, P. Fonagy, D. Cottrell, A. Cotgrove, and E. Boddington. 2004. Selective serotonin reuptake inhibitors in childhood depression: Systematic review of published versus unpublished data. *Lancet* 363:1341–45.

Widom, C.S. 1999. Post-traumatic stress disorder in abused and neglected children grown up. *American Journal of Psychiatry* 156:1223–29.

Wilcox, J.A. 1995. Divalproex sodium as a treatment for borderline personality disorder. *Annals of Clinical Psychiatry* 7:33–37.

Zanarini, M.C., and F.R. Frankenburg. 2001. Olanzapine treatment of female borderline personality disorder patients: A doubleblind, placebo-controlled pilot study. *Journal of Clinical Psychiatry* 62:849–54.

Zanarini, M.C., F.R. Frankenburg, J. Hennen, D.B. Reich, and K.R. Silk. 2004. Axis I comorbidity in patients with borderline personality disorder: Six-year follow-up and prediction of time to remission. *American Journal of Psychiatry* 161:2108–14.

Zanarini, M.C., F.R. Frankenburg, J. Hennen, and K.R. Silk. 2003. The longitudinal course of borderline psychopathology: Six-year prospective follow-up of the phenomenology of borderline personality disorder.

*American Journal of Psychiatry* 160:274–83.

Zanarini, M.C., F.R. Frankenburg, A.A. Vujanovic, J. Hennen, D.B. Reich, and K.R. Silk. 2004. Axis II comorbidity of borderline personality disorder: Description of six-year course and prediction to time-to-remission. *Acta Psychiatrica Scandinavica* 110:416–20.

Zanarini, M.C., J.G. Gunderson, M.F. Marino, E.O. Schwartz, and F.R. Frankenburg. 1988. DSM-III disorders in the families of borderline outpatients. *Journal of Personality Disorders* 2:292–302.

Zanarini, M.C., A.A. Williams, R.E. Lewis, R.B. Reich, S.C. Vera, M.F. Marino, A. Levin, L. Yong, and F.R. Frankenburg. 1997. Reported pathological childhood experiences associated with the development of borderline personality disorder. *American Journal of Psychiatry* 154:1101–6.

Zanarini, M.C., L. Yong, F.R. Frankenburg, J. Hennen, D.B. Reich, and M.F. Marino. 2002. Severity of reported childhood sexual abuse and its relationship to severity of borderline psychopathology and psychosocial impairment among borderline patients. *Journal of Nervous and Mental Disease* 190:381–87.

Zlotnick, C. 1997. Posttraumatic stress disorder (PTSD), PTSD comorbidity, and childhood abuse among incarcerated women. *Journal of Nervous and Mental Disease* 185:761–63.

**Alexander L. Chapman, Ph.D.,** is an assistant professor and a registered psychologist in the Department of Psychology at Simon Fraser University, where he conducts research on borderline personality disorder, emotion regulation, self-harm, and related topics. After graduating with his Ph.D. in clinical psychology from Idaho State University and completing a clinical internship at Duke University Medical Center, Chapman completed a two-year post-doctoral fellowship with Marsha Linehan at the University of Washington. While working with Linehan, he received training and supervision in dialectical behavior therapy (DBT) and in clinical research on borderline personality disorder. Chapman has published numerous journal articles and book chapters and has given many professional presentations on borderline personality disorder, suicidal and self-harm behavior, DBT, and impulsive behavior, among other topics. In 2007, Chapman was awarded the Young Investigator's Award of the National Education Alliance for Borderline Personality Disorder (NEA-BPD). He has also coauthored a book on behavior therapy. Chapman has had several years of experience and extensive training in the treatment of borderline personality disorder. He routinely gives workshops on DBT, consults with clinicians regarding the treatment of BPD in both Canada and the United States, teaches courses on DBT, and supervises students in their treatment of clients with BPD. In addition, Chapman founded the Dialectical Behaviour Therapy Centre of Vancouver (DBTCV), a center for the treatment of persons who struggle with BPD.

**Kim L. Gratz, Ph.D.,** is research assistant professor in the Department of Psychology at the University of Maryland, and director of the Personality Disorders Division of the Center for Addictions, Personality, and Emotion Research. Gratz received her Ph.D. in clinical psychology from the University of Massachusetts, Boston, in 2003, where her research focused on deliberate self-harm. She completed her pre-doctoral internship training, with an emphasis on the treatment of BPD, at McLean Hospital/Harvard Medical School.

In July 2003, she was awarded the Psychosocial Fellowship from McLean Hospital/Harvard Medical School. In her role as clinical and research fellow under the mentorship of John Gunderson, Gratz conducted a study examining the efficacy of a new emotion regulation group therapy for the treatment of self-harm among women with BPD and developed a research program to assess the effectiveness of the Borderline Center, McLean Hospital's specialty clinical services for BPD. During this time, she also served as a primary clinician within McLean Hospital's DBT program, providing individual and group DBT to clients with BPD and related disorders. Gratz joined the Clinical Psychology Program at the University of Maryland in 2005. She has written numerous journal articles and book chapters on BPD, deliberate self-harm, and emotion regulation (among other topics), and, in 2005, was awarded the Young Investigator's Award of the National Education Alliance for Borderline Personality Disorder (NEA-BPD). Her research currently focuses on understanding the nature and consequences of emotion dysregulation and emotional avoidance in BPD and self-harm, and applying this understanding to the development of more effective treatments for these conditions. In addition, Gratz will soon be opening a treatment clinic, specializing in the treatment of BPD, through the Center for Addictions, Personality, and Emotion Research at the University of Maryland.

www.ingramcontent.com/pod-product-compliance
Lightning Source LLC
Chambersburg PA
CBHW050323230426
43663CB00010B/1719